Edward Bond

Restoration

D0507090

B L O O M S B U R Y

LONDON • NEW DELHI • NEW YORK • SYDNEY

Bloomsbury Methuen Drama

An imprint of Bloomsbury Publishing Plc

50 Bedford Square	1385 Broadway
London	New York
WC1B 3DP	NY 10018
UK	USA

www.bloomsbury.com

Bloomsbury is a registered trade mark of Bloomsbury Publishing Plc

Published by Methuen Drama 2006

First published in Great Britain in 1981 in the Royal Court Writers Series by Eyre Methuen Ltd.
Revised and re-set in 1982 in the Methuen Modern Plays series by Methuen London Ltd.
Revised and published in 1992 for *Bond Plays: 4* by Methuen Drama
Revised and published in this edition in 2006 by Methuen Drama

Visit www.bloomsbury.com to find out more about our authors and their books
You will find extracts, author interviews, author events and you can sign up for
newsletters to be the first to hear about our latest releases and special offers.

British Library Cataloguing-in-Publication Data
A catalogue record for this book is available from the British Library.

ISBN: PB:	978-0-7136-8330-1
EPDF:	978-1-4081-7144-8
EPUB:	978-1-4081-6993-3

Library of Congress Cataloging-in-Publication Data
A catalog record for this book is available from the Library of Congress.

Headlong

Headlong Theatre
in association with Bristol Old Vic presents

RESTORATION

by Edward Bond

First performance of this production
on 7 September 2006 at Bristol Old Vic

Headlong Theatre

in association with Bristol Old Vic presents

RESTORATION

by Edward Bond

ROSE	Madeline Appiah
MR HARDACHE / PARSON	Robert East
MOTHER / LADY ARE	Beverley Klein
LORD ARE	Mark Lockyer
ANN / MRS WILSON	Dorothea Myer-Bennett
FRANK	Michael Shaeffer
BOB	Mark Stobbart
DIRECTOR	Rupert Goold
DESIGNER	Colin Richmond
LIGHTING DESIGNER	Oliver Fenwick
COMPOSER & SOUND DESIGNER	Adam Cork

For *Restoration*

Production Management	Paul Hennessy
	for The Production Desk
Company Stage Manager	Lizzie Dudley
Deputy Stage Manager	Julia Reid
Technical Assistant Stage Manager	Lucy McMahon
Musical Director	Tom Deering
Costume Supervisor	Freya Morris
Wig Supervisor	Madeline Heyer
Wardrobe Manager	Amy Brown
Re-Lighter/Production Electrician	Tom Snell
Assistant Director	Louise Simpson
Set build	Bristol Old Vic Scenic Workshops
Set transport	Southern Van Lines
Lighting hires	Stage Lighting Services
Sound hires	Stage Sound Services
Cloths	Gerriets GB
Production Insurance	Walton & Parkinson
Press & Marketing	Julia Hallawell
	for The Touring Team
Casting Director	Hannah Miller
Education Associate	Kelly Wilkinson
Production Photography	Manuel Harlan
Graphic Design	Eureka! (www.eureka.co.uk)

Acknowledgements

Theatre Royal Bury St Edmunds for permission to use
the poster image, National Theatre Costume Hire
and Paperchase

With special thanks to Natalie Abrahami

This play was first performed at the Royal Court Theatre,
London, on 21 July 1981

Edward Bond's *Restoration*

When the Lord Chamberlain stated in 1968 that Edward
Bond's play *Early Morning*, 'must not be performed', he
struck a tone of outrage and dismissal which has been
consistently levelled at the writer's work in the years
which have followed. Since his first two plays, *The Pope's
Wedding* and *Saved* premiered at the Royal Court over
thirty years ago, Bond has found himself standing in near-
solitary opposition to the mainstream in terms of both
the subject matter of his plays and the exposing ambition
of his tone and style. Bond is a writer who is determined
to excavate and investigate the harshest truths of our
society, constantly peeling back the veneer of civilisation
to reveal the violence and cruelty, the animalistic
impulsiveness, beneath. His plays are brutal, tender and
often almost unbearable to watch, such is the unflinching
directness with which their author drives his events and
characters through to their inevitable conclusion.

Restoration may appear, at first glance, to stand apart
from the Bond canon in terms of its humour, its
sophistication, its musicality. In fact, it represents perhaps
the purest expression of his vision. The more civilised
the veneer, the more coruscating the impact when it is
removed. What could be more elegantly sophisticated,
more intelligent and good-humoured, than the verbal
sparring and theatrical wit of a restoration comedy?
Bond shows us the bitter, barbaric struggle beneath the
comedy, the cruelty which is the engine powering this
world. The violence in *Restoration* may be less obvious,
less physical than in some of his more controversial
work, but its bloody rhythm pulses through every
moment of the drama. This is a play about death, about

imprisonment both actual and metaphorical, about the impossibility of freedom for those who find themselves born in the wrong place at the wrong time. The fact that it is funny, sometimes blissfully so, only underlines the uncomfortable truth which Bond so mercilessly pursues. Yes, we can laugh, but when we do so we should know that we laugh with the rich at the poor, with the winners at the losers, with the free at the imprisoned.

The two new songs, being heard for the first time in this production, examine further this investigation into freedom enjoyed and denied. The seventeenth-century characters in *Restoration* are trapped in a spiral of social oppression, the aristocracy triumphant, the poor driven toward the gallows. In the same way, the new songs reveal the spiral of violence in which the world finds itself caught in 2006, the inevitable march toward more blood and more dead. The rich of the first-world are now the prisoners, the hunted, the poor are become the repressors, the terrorists. Just as there is no hope for Bob Hedges in the play, unless he can truly understand that he is not a free man, so there is little hope for the world in 2006, whilst we 'don't know how to make peace'.

Ben Power
August 2006

Cast

MADELINE APPIAH (ROSE)

Training: Madeline trained at The Liverpool Institute of Performing Arts.
Theatre: Credits include Juliette *I Have Before Me A Remarkable Document Given To Me By A Young Lady From Rwanda* (Dublin Fringe), Isabella *Cinderella* (Watford Palace Theatre), Zina *Brezhnev's Children* (BAC), Young Diana Ross *Diana: The Lady and Her Music* (Neptune Theatre), Mrs Cricket *The Insect Play* (LIPA) Lucy *Redundant* (LIPA), Mark Anthony *Julius Caesar* (LIPA), Launce *Two Gentlemen Of Verona* (LIPA), Natasha *Plasticine* (LIPA).
TV: *EastEnders, The Bill, Holby City*.
Other: Madeline was nominated for best actress in the Dublin Fringe Festival for her role as Juilette in *I Have Before Me A Remarkable Document By A Young Lady From Rwanda*.

ROBERT EAST (MR HARDACHE / PARSON)

Training: Robert read English at Oxford University.
Theatre: London theatre includes *Journey's End* (New Ambassadors), *Stuff Happens* (National Theatre), *The Tempest* and *King Lear* (Old Vic), *Richard III* (Savoy), *Twelve Angry Men* (Comedy), *An Ideal Husband* (Old Vic), *The Hothouse* (Comedy), *Half The Picture* and *Fashion* (Tricycle), *The Sisters Rosensweig* (Old Vic), *Brand* (Aldwych), *Run For Your Wife* (Criterion), *The Common Pursuit* (Lyric, Hammersmith), *Are You Lonesome Tonight* (Phoenix), *Rosencrantz And Guildenstern Are Dead* and *The Real Inspector Hound* (Young Vic) and *The Hothouse* (Hampstead and Ambassadors). National tours include *The Constant Wife, Funny About Love, The Colour Of Justice, Travels With My Aunt, An Ideal Husband* and *Bedroom Farce*. Repertory theatre includes *The Clean House, The Tempest, Richard III, The Birthday Party* and *Don Juan* (all at the Crucible, Sheffield), *Heartbreak House* (Chichester), *Hamlet* (Northcott, Exeter), *Broken Glass* and *Equus* (Royal, Northampton), *Our Day Out* (Playhouse, Liverpool) and *Passion Play* (New Wolsey, Ipswich).
TV: includes *Charles II, The Pardoner's Tale, Blackadder, Heartbeat, Miss Marple, Yes Minister, Yes Prime Minister, Dave Allen At Large, Emma, Across The Lake, Oneupmanship, Rumpole, The Hothouse, Unexplained Laughter*.
Film: *Figures in a Landscape, Brothers and Sisters* and *Lost Illusions*.
Radio: includes *Straight Down The Middle, A Slice Of Life, A Far Cry From Brazil* and *Dear Penny*, all of which he also wrote, and *Going Wrong*, which he adapted.
Restoration is Robert's second appearance in an Edward Bond play. He was the Fourth Prisoner/Old Counsellor in *Lear*, directed by Jonathan Kent at the Crucible, Sheffield.

BEVERLEY KLEIN (MOTHER / LADY ARE)

Training: Beverley graduated from the University of Warwick with a degree in English and American Literature.

Theatre: Credits include *Candide, Summerfolk. Romeo and Juliet, Honk,* the *Ugly Duckling, The Villain's Opera* (National Theatre); *Sweeney Todd* (Opera North); *How To Succeed in Business Without Really Trying, Six Pictures of Lee Miller* (Chichester Festival Theatre); *The Holy Terror* (Duke of York's); *The Woman Who Cooked Her Husband* (Snarling Beasties); *The Threepenny Opera* (Donmar Warehouse); *Sarrasine, Night After Night, A Judgement in Stone* (Gloria Theatre Co.); *Piaf* (Oldham Coliseum); *Les Miserables* (Barbican/ Palace Theatre); *Happy End* (Nottingham Playhouse); *Company* (Manchester Library); *Jerry Springer, The Opera* (Edinburgh Festival); *Fiddler on the Roof* (WYP); *Six Characters Looking For An Author* (Young Vic).
TV: *Gimme, Gimme, Gimme; Casualty; Down To Earth; Doctors; Dressing For Breakfast; Absolutely; Paris; The Hello Girls; Inspector Morse*; and *The Bill*
Film: *Came Out, It Rained, Went Back in Again.*
Other: Beverley has worked for several opera companies: *HMS Pinafore, Pirates of Penzance, Die Fledermaus* (Carl Rosa); *The Threepenny Opera* (Scottish Opera); *Arms and the Cow* (Opera North); *The Magic Flute* (MTL).

MARK LOCKYER (LORD ARE)

Training: Mark trained at RADA.
Theatre: Credits include: *Talk of the Devil* (Watford Palace Theatre); *Jane Eyre, The Alchemist, Peter Pan, Saved, Julius Caesar* (Birmingham Rep); *Carmen* (Derby Playhouse); *Twelfth Night* (Bristol Old Vic); *The Ragged Trousered Philanthropists* (Liverpool Playhouse/Theatre Royal Stratford East); *Outbreak of God in Area 9, Peribanez, The Adventures of Tintin* (Young Vic Theatre); *The Prisoner of Zenda* (Greenwich Theatre); *Hamlet, The Antipodes* (Globe); *The Clink* (Riverside Studios); *Othello, The Merchant of Venice, King Lear, The Tempest, Romeo and Juliet, The Taming of the Shrew, The Cherry Orchard* (Royal Shakespeare Company); *Bonjour la Bonjour, Living With the Lights On, The Whores of Babylon* (NT Studio); *Theatre of Blood, The Madness of George III, The Changeling, Ghetto, Fuente Ovejuna* (National Theatre).
TV: Credits include *The Fall of Rome, Joking Apart, The Great Kandinsky, The Bill, Chancer, Casualty, Out of Order.*
Radio: Credits include *The Minotaur, The Way of the World.*

DOROTHEA MYER-BENNETT (ANN / MRS WILSON)

Training: Dorothea trained at Bristol Old Vic Theatre School.
Theatre: Since graduating Dorothea played Fanny Mendelssohn in *Mendelssohn in Scotland* (Reading Hexagon and Royal Concert Hall Glasgow). While at drama school her roles included Dorinda in *The Beaux' Stratagem,* the Nurse in *Romeo and Juliet* and Audrey in *Blue Remembered Hills.*
TV: Arabella in *Jude the Obscure* (Dead Man Talking BBC)
Film: Feature: Tanya in *Checkmate* (Thema Productions, dir Olivier Bonas). Short: *Lucy in Ladies,* dir Carol Stevens.
Other: Voice over: *He/She, Veiled, Eclectic Films* (Cardiff Screen Festival)

MICHAEL SHAEFFER (FRANK)

Training: Michael trained at Rose Bruford College.
Theatre: Includes *Of Mice and Men* (Colchester Mercury); *Hamlet* (Royal Theatre, Northampton); *The Threepenny Opera* (National Theatre); *Original Sin* (Sheffield Crucible); *Macbeth* (Southwark Playhouse); *The Beautiful Game* (Cambridge Theatre); *Jesus Christ Superstar* (National Tour); *Oliver!* (London Palladium).
TV: *Kings and Queens, EastEnders, World in Arms – Navies*
Film: *Breaking and Entering* (Anthony Minghella), *Kingdom of Heaven* (Ridley Scott), *Matinee Queen, The Stain* and *The Sandwich.*

MARK STOBBART (BOB)

Training: Mark trained at Mountview Theatre School.
Theatre: Credits include *Up On the Roof* (Chichester); *The Lion, The Witch and the Wardrobe* (RSC); *Hello Again* (Bridewell); *Napoleon* (Shaftesbury); *War and Peace* (NT Studio); *People who don't do Dinner Parties* (Jermyn Street Theatre); *Let Him Have Justice* (Cochrane).
TV: *55 Degrees North, Little Britain, Auf Wiedersehen Pet, Inspector Lynley Mysteries, The Last Detective, Closes, All About Me.*

Creative Team

RUPERT GOOLD (Director)

Rupert Goold is Artistic Director of Headlong Theatre. Productions for Headlong include *Restoration* and *Paradise Lost*. From 2002-5 Rupert was Artistic Director of the Royal and Derngate Theatres in Northampton where productions included *Hamlet, Othello, Waiting for Godot, Insignificance, The Weir, Betrayal, Arcadia* and *Summer Lightning*. He was Associate Artist at Salisbury Playhouse from 1996-97 during its reopening under Jonathan Church where he directed *The End of the Affair, Dancing at Lughnasa* and the national tour of *Travels With My Aunt*. He was a Trainee Director under Sam Mendes at the Donmar Warehouse 1995-96. His work as a freelance director includes the world premiere of *Speaking Like Magpies*, a new play by Frank McGuinness, for the RSC; a national and international tour of *Scaramouche Jones* with Pete Postlethwaite, and in August 2006 he directed *The Tempest* with Patrick Stewart as Prospero for the RSC. His opera work includes *Le Comte Ory* (Garsington Opera) and *L'Opera Seria, Gli Equivoci* and *Il Pomo D'Oro* (Batignano). He will direct *Donna Del Largo* for Garsington Opera in 2007.

COLIN RICHMOND (Designer)

Colin trained at the Royal Welsh College of Music and Drama gaining First Class BA Hons in Theatre Design and The Lord Williams Award for Design two years running. 2003 Linbury Prize for Theatre Design Finalist and a Resident Designer as part of the Royal Shakespeare Company's Trainee Programme 2004-2005. Recent productions include: *L'Opera Seria* (Batignano Opera Festival (Tuscany), *Human Rites* (Southwark Playhouse), *Speakeasy* (Sherman Theatre Cardiff), *Hansel and Gretel* (Northampton Theatre Royal), *Lowdat* (Birmingham Rep), Beckett Double Bill *Play / Not I* (BAC) (winning design JMK young directors award) *Twelfth Night* (West Yorkshire Playhouse), *Breakfast with Mugabe* directed by Anthony Sher (Swan Theatre, RSC, Soho Theatre, Duchess, West End), *Bolt Hole* (Birmingham Rep), *House of the Gods* (Music Theatre Wales). *Bad Girls - the Musical* (West Yorkshire Playhouse) Future work includes *Shadow of a Gunman* (Glasgow Citizens Theatre) and a new one act opera by Jonathan Dove (London/ Italy).

Television includes assistant production designer (set) *Doctor Who*, BBC Wales (pre-production and series one).

OLIVER FENWICK (Lighting Designer)

Theatre credits include *Mirandolina* (Royal Exchange); *Comedy of Errors* (Crucible Theatre, Sheffield); *Dr. Faustus* (Liverpool Playhouse); *The Doll's House* (West Yorkshire Playhouse); *Fields of Gold* (Stephen Joseph Theatre); *The Solid Gold Cadillac* (Garrick Theatre); *Misconceptions* (Tour); *Insignificance, Breaking the Code* (Theatre Royal, Northampton); *Tartuffe, The Gentleman From Olmedo, The Venetian Twins, Hobson's Choice, Dancing at Lughnasa,* (Watermill Theatre); *Children of a Lesser God* (Salisbury Playhouse); *Caitlin, A Special Relationship* (York Theatre Royal); *Cinderella* (Bristol Old Vic); *The Secret Rapture* (West End); *Bird Calls, Iphigenia* (Crucible Theatre, Sheffield); *Old Ladies* (UK tour); *The Picture of Dorian Gray* (UK tour); *Old World* (UK tour); *Hysteria* (Salisbury Playhouse); *And All The Children Cried* (New End Theatre);*The Three Sisters, Wild Wild Women, The Daughter in Law* (Orange Tree Theatre, Richmond).

Opera credits include: *Samson et Delilah, Lohengrin* (Royal Opera House); *The Trojan Trilogy* (Linbury ROH); *The Little Magic Flute* (Opera North); *The Threepenny Opera* (for the Opera Group); *The Nose,* a Shostakovich opera (Lyric Hammersmith/Buxton Theatres).

ADAM CORK (Composer and Sound Designer)

Adam Cork read music at Cambridge University, studying composition with Robin Holloway.

Theatre: includes scores and sound designs for *Don Carlos* (Gielgud); *Suddenly Last Summer* (Albery); *Caligula, Henry IV, The Wild Duck, The Cut* (Donmar Warehouse); *On the Third Day* (New Ambassadors, subject of Channel 4 documentary *The Play's the Thing*); *Speaking Like Magpies, The Tempest* (RSC); *Five Gold Rings, The Late Henry Moss* (Almeida); *On The Ceiling* (Garrick); *Scaramouche Jones* (Riverside Studios and world tour); *Troilus and Cressida* (Old Vic); *Sunday Father* (Hampstead Theatre); *Nine Parts of Desire* (Wilma Theatre Philadelphia); *A Midsummer Night's Dream, Lear* (Sheffield Crucible); *Romeo*

and Juliet (Manchester Royal Exchange); *The Government Inspector* (Chichester Festival); *King Lear* (Chichester Minerva); *My Uncle Arly* (Royal Opera House Linbury); *The Field* (Tricycle Theatre); *Alice's Adventures in Wonderland* (Bristol Old Vic, received 2005 TMA Award Best Show for Young People); *Paradise Lost* (Oxford Stage Company). Adam was nominated for the 2005 Olivier Award for Best Sound Design for *Suddenly Last Summer* (Albery).
Film/TV: includes *Frances Tuesday* (ITV1), *Re-ignited* (Channel 4), *Bust* (Film Council), *Sexdrive* (Vancouver Film Festival), *Tripletake* (JJC Films)
Radio: includes *Losing Rosalind, The Luneberg Variation* (BBC Radio 4), *The Colonel-Bird* (BBC World Service), *Don Carlos* (BBC Radio 3).

TOM DEERING (Musical Director)

Tom studied music at Goldsmiths College, University of London, and then furthered his studies in piano and conducting at the Royal Academy of Music. Musical Director credits include: *Parade* (UK Premiere) *Southside; The Tinderbox* (Gardner Arts Centre)*; Carousel* (for Mountview at Bridewell Theatre); *Company (*Broadway Studio Theatre); *Other Women* (Bridewell Theatre); *Hot Mikado* (Wycombe Swan Theatre); *Passage of Dreams & Still Life* (Bridewell Theatre); *Goblin Market* (Lyric Theatre, Belfast – NYMT); *NewsRevue (*Canal Café Theatre); *Have a Nice Life* (Pleasance Theatre, London); *Jesus Christ Superstar* (Bloomsbury Theatre). As assistant musical director: *Nine* (Sir Jack Lyons Theatre); *Merrily We Roll Along* (Edinburgh Festival); *The Late Sleepers* (Newcastle Theatre Royal - NYMT). Tom has also played piano/keyboards on various shows including: *Billy Elliot* (Victoria Palace Theatre); *Mamma Mia!* (Prince Edward and Prince of Wales Theatres); *Just So, Out of This World, How to Succeed in Business Without Really Trying, Carousel,* (Chichester Festival Theatre); *The Snowman* (Peacock Theatre); *Jason Robert Brown* (New Players Theatre).
Original Cast Albums include: *Have a nice life* (MD & piano), *Goblin Market* (conductor) and *Just so* (piano & keyboard). Television and Radio include: *Frances Tuesday* (ITV1), *Who do they think they are?* (BBC2) and *Voice of Musical Theatre 2006* (BBC TV & Radio).

HANNAH MILLER (Casting Director)

Hannah is currently resident Casting Director for Birmingham Repertory Theatre where productions include *The Life of Galileo, Only the Lonely* by Nick Stafford, *The Wizard of Oz, Three Sisters* (Eclipse Theatre Initiative), *Pravda* and *To Kill a Mockingbird.* Previously she was Deputy Casting Director at the RSC and Casting Assistant at the National Theatre. Other work includes *Arcadia* and *The Importance of Being Earnest* (Northampton Theatres), *Kalila wa Dimna* by Sulayman al-Bassam (The Pit, Barbican and world tour), *Visible* by Sarah Woods (Cardboard Citizens) and a gala reading of Treatment Theatre's *Who Killed Mr Drum* (Old Vic).

Headlong Theatre

The new name for Oxford Stage Company

HEADLONG: /hedl'ong/ *noun* 1. with head first,
2. starting boldly, 3. to approach with speed and vigour

Headlong Theatre is dedicated to new ways of making theatre. By exploring revolutionary writers and practitioners of the past and commissioning new work from artists from a wide variety of backgrounds we aim constantly to push the imaginative boundaries of the stage. **Headlong** makes exhilarating, provocative and spectacular new work to take around the country and around the world.

> *'... one of the great success stories of recent years'*
> The Daily Telegraph

Artistic Director	Rupert Goold
Executive Producer	Henny Finch
Finance Manager	Helen Hillman
Literary Associate	Ben Power
Administrator / Trainee Producer	Jenni Kershaw

For more information or to join our mailing list, please go to
www.headlongtheatre.co.uk

Chertsey Chambers, 12 Mercer Street,
London, WC2H 9QD

Tel 020 7438 9940   *Fax* 020 7438 9941

Headlong Theatre is supported by

ARTS COUNCIL
ENGLAND

Bristol Old Vic

*'Apologies for the déjà vu you're bound to experience in reading
that Bristol Old Vic has, once again, excelled itself.'*
Daily Telegraph, 2006

Bristol Old Vic is enjoying a renaissance in its fortunes. It produces award-winning and critically acclaimed classics and new works, a wide range of shows for families, as well as experimental work in its studio theatre. The company also enjoys collaborations with a wide range of national and regional companies of all scales, and is delighted to be working with Headlong Theatre on this production.

Since 2003, Bristol Old Vic's award-winning productions have included *A Midsummer Night's Dream, Paradise Lost, Private Peaceful, Alice's Adventures in Wonderland* and *Beasts and Beauties* – *'The first night audience did not exit from the theatre, they hover-crafted out of it on a balloon of bliss.'* (The Independent on *Beasts and Beauties*).

This autumn there are major new productions of *The Birthday Party*, starring the legendary comedy actress, Sheila Steafel, a radical version of Marlowe's *Doctor Faustus* directed and designed by David Fielding and a bold multi-media production of *Macbeth*. And at Christmas, Bristol Old Vic presents a specially commissioned version of *The Three Musketeers* by West End and Broadway writer Ken Ludwig.

Bristol Old Vic's home is a gorgeous Georgian auditorium in the city's harbourside. While audiences have been coming non-stop since 1766, the building is now in desperate need of repair. Plans for the immediate future include a major refurbishment campaign, to be launched in autumn 2006.

Artistic Director   Simon Reade
Administrative Director   Rebecca Morland

Tickets 0117 987 7877   *Online* www.bristol-old-vic.co.uk

King Street, Bristol, BS1 4ED, UK

Restoration

Edward Bond was born and educated in London. His plays
include *The Pope's Wedding* (Royal Court Theatre, 1962), *Saved*
(Royal Court, 1965), *Early Morning* (Royal Court, 1968), *Lear*
(Royal Court, 1971), *The Sea* (Royal Court, 1973), *The Fool*
(Royal Court, 1975), *The Woman* (National Theatre, 1978),
Restoration (Royal Court, 1981), *Summer* (National Theatre,
1982), *The War Plays* (RSC at the Barbican Pit, 1985), *In the
Company of Men* (Paris, 1992; RSC at the Barbican Pit, 1996),
At the Inland Sea (toured by Big Brum Theatre-in-Education,
1995), *Coffee* (Rational Theatre Company, Cardiff and
London, 1996; Paris, 2000), *Eleven Vests* (toured by Big Brum
Theatre-in-Education, 1997), *The Crime of the Twenty-first
Century* (published 1998 and produced in Paris, 2000), *The
Children* (Classworks, Cambridge, 2000), *Have I None* (toured by
Big Brum Theatre-in-Education, 2000), *Existence* (Paris, 2002),
The Under Room (toured by Big Brum Theatre-in-Education,
2005) and *Born* (Avignon, 2006); also *Olly's Prison* (BBC2
Television, 1993), *Tuesday* (BBC Schools TV, 1993) and *Chair*
(BBC Radio 4, 2000).

Restoration was first presented at the Royal Court Theatre, London, on 21 July 1981, with the following cast:

Bob	Philip Davis
Lord Are	Simon Callow
Frank	Nicholas Ball
Mr Hardache	Wolfe Morris
Parson	Norman Tyrrell
Gabriel	John Barrett
Messenger	Kit Jackson
Gaoler	Patrick Murray
Rose	Debbie Bishop
Mother (Mrs Hedges)	Elizabeth Bradley
Ann	Eva Griffith
Mrs Wilson	Darlene Johnson
Old Lady Are	Irene Handl

Directed by	Edward Bond
Music by	Nick Bicât
Designed by	Hayden Griffin
	and Gemma Jackson
Lighting by	Rory Dempster

Characters

Lord Are
Frank
Bob Hedges
Mr Hardache
Ann
Rose
Mother (Mrs Hedges)
Parson
Gaoler
Mrs Wilson
Old Lady Are
Messenger

Time

The eighteenth century

Place

England – or another place at another time

Part One

Part Two

Part One

It's a big broad fine sunny day
The black clouds are gonna blow away
It's true that the rockets are aimed in their pits
But they won't be fired, not this time
This time there ain't gonna be any crime
This time we're gonna say no
This time we're gonna be wise guys
And tell the bastards where to go

It's a big broad fine sunny day
It's getting more sunny all the time
It's true that the bombs are stacked in their racks
But we won't load them up, not this time
This time there ain't gonna be no more war
This time we're gonna say no
This time we're gonna be wise guys
And tell the bastards where to go

It's a big broad fine sunny day
It's getting better all the time
And this time the soldiers will not march away
So they won't be shot at, not this time
This time they ain't gonna die for the sods
This time they're gonna say no
This time they're staying here to play
And tell the bastards where to go

It's a big broad fine sunny day
And the sky gets bluer all the time
From now on we'll live in the way that we say
And we won't be told, not this time
This is our world and it's staying that way
This time we're gonna say no
Today we'll live till tomorrow
And tell the bastards where to go

Scene One

London, the park of **Lord Are**'*s house.*

Are *and* **Frank**. **Frank** *is in livery.*

Are   Lean me against that great thing.

Frank   The oak sir?

Are   Hold your tongue. No no! D'ye want me to appear drunk? Nonchalant. As if I often spent the day leaning against an oak or supine in the grass.

Frank   Your lordship comfortable?

Are   No scab I am not, if that gives ye joy. Hang my scarf over the twig. Delicately! – as if some discriminating wind had cast it there. Stand off. How do I look?

Frank   Well sir . . . how would yer like to look?

Are   Pox! Ye city vermin can't tell the difference between a haystack and a chimney stack. Wha-ha! I must not laugh, it'll spoil my pose. Damn! The sketch shows a flower. 'Tis too late for the shops, I must have one from the ground.

Frank   What kind sir?

Are   Rip up that pesky little thing on the path. That'll teach it to grow where gentlemen walk.

Frank *offers the flower.*

Are   Smell it! If it smells too reprehensible throw it aside. I hate the gross odours the country gives off. 'Tis always in a sweat! Compare me to the sketch.

Frank (*checks sketch*)   Leg a bit more out.

Are   Lawd I shall be crippled. *Do* they stand about the country so? When I pass the boundaries of the town I lower the blinds in mourning and never go out on my estate for fear of the beasts.

Frank   Cows aren't beasts sir.

Are The peasants sirrah. Don't mar the sketch with your great thumbs. I had it drew up by a man renowned for his landscapes to show me how a gentleman drapes himself across his fields. That I call a proper use for art. The book oaf! Well sirrah open it! Must I gaze on the cover as if I wondered what manner of thing I held in my hand?

Frank Any page sir?

Are The blanker the better. (*Looks at the page.*) Turn sir. The poet spilt his ink and scribbled to use it up before it dried. A poem should be well cut and fit the page neatly as if it were written by your tailor. The secret of literary style lies in the margins. Now *that* sir could only have been written by Lord Lester's tailor, whose favourite colour is woad. Turn me to something short. Your master is a man of epigrammatic wit. About your business. I must pine.

Frank *goes.*

Are What a poor gentleman I am! Town house and park, country house and land as far as the eye can see – they tell me – debts to honour a duke, and broke. So: a rich bride. Yonder, about to rise over the horizon like a pillar of smoke, is Mr Hardache, iron founder, shipbuilder, mine owner and meddler and merchant in men and much else that hath money in it. With his daughter, who must have a title and country estate to go with her fortune. So here I am set, imitating the wild man of the woods. An extravagant gesture, but I would have the gal love me at sight and be spared the tedium of courting an ironmaster's daughter. Faith boys what would one do: rattle a spoon in a tin mug and call it a serenade? Peace good soul! You have but to glance up from this bundle of tasteless moralising – the relief itself will bring rapture to thy face – and the slut's fate is sealed. I hope I am not to wait for a change in the season? I shall put out branches or turn white in a hoar frost.

Bob *enters.*

Are A swain wanders o'er the landscape.

Bob   Well London here I am! What strange sights I hev seen!

Are   Why does the fool gawp so impertinently? Lawd it grins!

Bob   Mornin' my lord.

Are   Gad it addresseth me! Oaf be off!

Bob   Ay sir where to?

Are   Where to? What care I where to? To hell! Wha-ha!
(*Aside.*) Dear heart do not discommode thy complexion. A raw
face is a countrified look but I would not have one even to gaze
the blazing of the bankruptcy court! Dear gad my foot is
misplaced!

Bob (*aside*)   Doo a London gentleman complain when his foot
move? However do they git into bed – or out of it?

Are (*aside*)   I am dealing with a harmless lunatic. The iron
people have turned into the avenue. Soon we shall hear them
clank. – Good fellow, take the run of my grounds. Go and
play.

Bob (*aside*)   This is a test Bob. Don't git caught out. (*Idea.*)
Drat what a fool I am! That owd rag round your neck hev
hitched yoo up in the bramble! Tell by the look on yoor face!
I'll soon haul yoo out sir!

Are (*pushing* **Bob** *away*)   Off sir! Back to your bedlam!

Bob   Why sir, 'tis Bob – come of age and sent up to serve as
yoor man, as laid down in the history of our estate: eldest
Hedges boy hev the right to serve his lord.

Are (*aside*)   This comes from opening a poetry book. –
Sirrah . . . ?

Bob   Bob sir. Or Robert Hedges.

Are   Bob, yonder is a paddock. Go and graze.

Bob   Graze sir?

Are   A country lad must know how to graze!

Bob (*aside*)   I must learn their ways if I'm to survive. – Ay sir.

Are   Then graze.

Bob (*shrugs. Aside*)   I'll chew three stalks t' show willin'. That'll hev to doo.

Bob *goes.*

Are   Yonder comes my money. (*Reads.*)

Hardache *enters.*

Hardache   Lord Are.

Are   La sir ye surprised me!

Hardache   My girl's back of the hedge, studyin' the shop window. (*Calls.*) Come daughter, or his lordship'll think you don't know your manners. – A retiring lass.

Are (*aside*)   Good. Let her retire to the country and leave London to me.

Hardache   You'll soon know her ways. Mind she has a temper – like her mother. That blessed woman ran my shops like an empire. (*Calls.*) Pst! Come daughter. – She has all the airs of a lady. Last week the soup was cold. She hauls the cook in and rows her out in front of the guests till she shakes like a dog being shown the well. Anything she likes, she must have. Saw a carriage with a new fancy way of panels – must have. A duchess with diamonds in her hat – must have. Skrawky pet dog – must have. Little black maid – one of them too. I don't begrudge. She's all that's left of her mother to me, barrin' a few shawls. That good woman worked all her life – till we had a penny to spend on ourselves and tuppence to mend the damage – and died at the counter with a slice of dinner in her hand. We're a family sort of family –

Are (*aside*)   Lawd he'll quote me the jingles on his family tombstones.

Hardache   – and I intend to make you part of us!

Are (*aside*)   Pox if I call him father!

Ann (*off*)   Pst!

Hardache   You call my sweet?

Are   Fetch her sir – (*Aside.*) 'ere the ivy grow o'er me.

Hardache (*calls*)   I'll meet you halfway.

Ann *comes on downstage and* **Hardache** *goes down to her.*

Are   Not uncomely, but the neglect is beyond redemption!
Style cannot strike at any age like a conversion. Its rudiments
are learned in the nursery or never. That redness of cheek
might be had off a coster's barrow for ha'pence. But I'll take
her, as she comes with money.

Hardache   Well sweetheart? (*By her.*) Hussy you're fit for
nowt but an errand boy but you're my daughter and you'll
marry an earl.

Ann   But Father! He's got four limbs and his wind. He could
last for years.

Hardache   Shan't I buy good stock?

Ann   O you are a fool Father! Lucy's old baron died of over-
eating in a year – and he was no trouble while he were alive.
He chased her round the bed but were too fat to catch her. She
lost pounds and looked better after her marriage than she did
before – and few girls can say as much!

Hardache   Come miss.

Ann   Even that ugly Mary Flint. Her father got her an earl of
nowt but twenty-five. But he was so eaten up with the diseases
he was born with and those he'd acquired – and mad, she had
three doctors testify to him before she signed the settlement –
that when they came into church the poor parson didn't know
whether to turn to the marriage ceremony or the burial of the
dead. He were right too: they'd no sooner left the church than
they had to go back for the interment. She went with the
pealing and came back with the tolling. But what have you
ever done for me Father?

Hardache   Presently my lord!

Ann   You are a thoughtless man.

Are   Pray unhitch me.

Ann   Can't we leave him to see if he hang?

Hardache (*to* **Are**)   My daughter's too well brought up to touch a gentleman's linen in public. (*Releases* **Are**.) Now sir.

Are   Servant ma'am.

Ann   Good day sir. (*Aside.*) Perhaps he's prone to accidents. – Did the scarf wound you sir?

Are   Wound! Fwa! when I take a toss out hunting the ground cracks.

Ann (*aside*)   Well, best know the worst. He's still the first box at the play, eating out in great houses, orchestral balls. I'll be presented at court and dance with the prince the second time he asks – the first time I'll be in one of my pets and give him a great yawn.

Are (*aside*)   Cupid has lodged his shaft. I'll beat up my price and set her onto that old maker of cinders. That light in the eye of a slut or a countess is the true lust for money.

Hardache (*calls*)   Rose! – You youngsters go and look at the flowers. I'll wait up at the house.

Are *and* **Ann** *go.*

Rose *comes in.*

Hardache   Call me if the hussy runs off. He can fondle her hand and rub up against her – but nowt else.

Rose   Yes sir.

Hardache *goes.* **Bob** *comes on. He has already met* **Rose**.

Bob   Hev you notice the sky is gold? Knew the street ont paved with it. If I was towd the sky was I ont believe that neither.

Rose   The sun shines on the smoke.

Bob   Lawd. I'm Bob. What yoo called gal?

Rose   Rose.

Bob   Will you show us London Rose?

Rose   Won't get time for sightseein'.

Bob   I intend to see the churches an' palaces an' docks an' markets. Whey-hay! Rose, if yoor lady an' my lord git wed, as yoo say, us'll see a lot of each other, which us'll like. Make a bargain: yoo say everytime I goo wrong.

Rose   That'll keep me busy. You run up here to get away from some poor cow carryin' your bastard.

Bob   Thass a lie! Ont ought a charge a chap with that!

Rose   Keep yer shirt on.

Bob   Thass all right then s'long as we know. – Look at the way *they* go on! Could drive a cart between 'em. I'll show yoo how that ought to be done. First yoo take the gal's hand an' walk her up an' down. Bin a hard week so she soon git tired an' goo a bit slow. He's a thoughtful chap so he steer her to a bank an' pat the grass. 'Take the weight off yoor feet gal.'

Rose   No I'm wearing my best dress.

Bob   Yoo hev t'say yes or I can't show yoo how to doo it. 'Look' he say 'yoo're a pretty gal' an' he give her a – (*Picks up* **Are***'s flower.*) Lady's Smock. Then yoo give him a kiss.

Rose   Why?

Bob   You hev to!

Rose   Why?

Bob   God yoo're a disconcertin' woman, gal! Thass considered very rude in Hilgay. Yoo hev the flower, yoo hev t'kiss – or thass bad luck for both parties for a whole year. Ought to give us some luck Rose – (*Kisses her.*) on my first day in London.

ROSES (**Bob**)

I lay a red rose on your breast
A red rose on a dusky flower
It rises and falls in the scent of your mouth
Your breath is a breeze that blows
In the silent world where the ice walls tower
And melts the snows to sparkling streams
And brings the swallows home from the south . . .
In the scent of your breath and from the rose
The petals open and fall apart
Scatter and lie upon your heart
And there I lay my head in repose
I kiss the petals
They stir and close
Close to the secret bud again
The bud in which are hidden away
The breezes of spring
The gentle rain
And the warmth of a summer's day.

Scene Two

Hilgay. The Hall. Porch.

Mother *and* **Parson**.

Mother   Upset yoo onto let 'em parade in a line. Ont often git a bit of fun.

Parson   Let them work – that's what his lordship would wish to see.

Are *and* **Ann** *enter.*

Frank *goes in and out with boxes.*

Are   Faw! The dust! Parson ye have emptied your graveyard on my doorstep!

Parson   My lord I shall pray for rain.

Are *enters the house.*

Ann   Every bone in my body's broken. (*To* **Frank**.) Mind that box man!

Parson   My lady welcome to Hilgay. We asked a blessing on the wedding –

Ann (*to* **Frank**)   Get them away from his feet!

Parson   – and would gladly have held the service at St John's. His lordship's father was christened, married and buried there, as were –

Ann (*to* **Frank**)   Don't slam it man!

Frank   'S heavy.

Ann   So will my fist be round your chops!

Mother   M'lady Mrs Hedges, yoor housekeeper.

Ann   Who are those ruffians loitering round the back?! Be off! They'll steal my new things!

Bob *comes in. His livery is the same as* **Frank**'s.

Parson   My lady the parish has had an outbreak of Methodists! On Sunday I took the horses from their stalls and drove the fanatics through the lanes.

Ann *goes in. The* **Parson** *follows.*

Bob   Ma.

Mother   Boy yoo look smart.

They can't embrace because **Bob** *is putting down a parcel.*

Bob   Keepin' well?

Mother   Gittin' by. She the sort a creature she looks like?

Bob   Yes if thass cow.

Mother   I can handle cows.

Bob *goes in.* **Mother** *examines the luggage.*

Mother   Huh load of old stuff. Ont need that here.

Rose *comes in.* **Mother** *straightens up and sees her.*

Mother   Eek!

Rose   Mrs Hedges.

Mother   Thought the devil catch me pryin'. Give me a turn gal.

Rose   I'm the lady's maid.

Mother   Ay. Heard the London servants was getting black. Sorry I shouted my dear. The house is my territory by right and conquest. What goo on outside come under the steward or head gardener – I ont responsible for their lawlessness. Mr Phelps is the parson when yoo goo to church – which yoo better had, doo they complain – an' the magistrate when yoo goo to court – which you better hadn't. Yoor regular duties come under her ladyship but anything relatin' to the runnin' of the house come under me: where yoo sit at table, upkeep of yoor room an' any set-to yoo hev with the servants – I'm the law, an' the mercy if yoo're lucky. That clear my pet? Disorder's unprofitable all round.

Rose   Ta I like to know where I am.

Mother   Git her ladyship settled like a good gal and come down to my kitchen. (*Idea.*) Yoo ont eat special?

Rose   No.

Mother   Jist as well 'cause we ont hev it. I'll find yoo summat tasty.

Bob *comes in and embraces* **Rose**.

Mother   You two know each other.

Rose   We're married Mrs Hedges.

Mother   Married! Well. (*Pause for thought.*) Black cow give milk same as white cow. They say black the grate an' the fire burn better. Still, God doo goo in for surprises. Hev a daughter-in-law! Well send a lad to London he's bound to come back different.

Bob   We're very happy Ma.

Mother   They all are t' start with, otherwise they ont git married. Well. Us'll hev to. Fancy hevin' a daughter! Take a minute to git use to! Need a double bed. I'll invite both on yoo to a glass of wine in my pantry. Settle her ladyship first. On't want a paddy on her first day in the house.

Rose   Let the cow wait.

Frank *comes in.*

Frank   Nobs gone up?

Rose   Yeh.

Frank   Dump ennit? Don't yer get lost? 'Fraid to stick me head out the winder 'case I can't find me way back. Do all right though! What's the talent like? Smart lad down from London, good-looker, spin a yarn, knocked about a bit – what? Answer to a maiden's prayer. Yoo bin prayin' Ma? 'Ere, yoo speak English or do animal imitations like Bob?

Mother   Mrs Hedges the housekeeper. Pleased to make yoor acquaintance, Mr . . . ?

Frank   Frank love, I dispense with the title. All them bulls an' cows runnin' abaht in the altogether – gals must go round ready for it all the time. But I don't fancy them fields. Now a back alley's been the scene of many of my –

Bob   Pay no notice.

Frank   Speaks English though don't she Bobby? Well sort of. She yer ma? Pleased to meet yer Mrs Hedges.

Mother   If they bought a donkey for its bray I could sell yoo to the Lord Mayor. Git all that stuff out my porch –

Frank   Your ma gettin' at me, Bobby?

Mother   – before we break our necks.

Frank   Not me Mrs Hedges. I'm the outdoor servant. Bob's indoors. I fetch an' carry outside – *an'* not all this junk. In London it's letters, presents done up in little boxes, pick up from the florists, or follow yer lady when she's shoppin'. If this was London an' his lordship stood on that line I'd have to clean the front of his boots an' Bobby'd have to clean the back.

SONG OF LEARNING (**Frank**)

For fifty thousand years I lived in a shack
I learned that a shack is not a place to live in
For fifty thousand years I built mansions for men of wealth
That's how I learned to build a mansion for myself

For fifty thousand years I printed their books
I learned how to read by looking over their shoulder
For fifty thousand years I built libraries for men of wealth
That's how I learned to write the books I need for myself

For fifty thousand years I fought in their wars
I died so often I learned how to survive
For fifty thousand years I fought battles to save their wealth
That's how I learned to know the enemy myself

I have known pain and bowed before beauty
Shared in joy and died in duty
Fifty thousand years I lived well
I learned how to blow up your hell

Scene Three

*Hilgay. The Hall. Lady **Are**'s drawing room.*

Ann *with a book.*

Ann   Last night I had a wonderful dream. We were walking arm in arm. A perfect day. Suddenly rain bucketed down. We sheltered under a tree. Wind howled in the branches – and a bolt of lightning hit it. It crashed down, struck my husband on the head and drove him straight into the ground like a hammer striking a nail. He weren't there! Vanished! Killed and buried at one blow! I wasn't even brushed. Then the sun came out. Well it would wouldn't it? And Lucy and Peg – my best school chums – rode up in a carriage sat on top of a great mountain of my luggage. And I'm whisked off to a gala given by royalty at Covent Garden for all the people to celebrate my release. Ee I was that happy!

Are *comes in. He carries bills.* **Ann** *curtsies.*

Are   If ye've crooked your ankle try cow liniment ma'am.

Ann (*aside*)   I shan't be provoked. – O what a lovely thing!

Are   What ma'am?

Ann   That jacket.

Are   D'ye like it? My plum red. Ye begin to have taste.

Ann   And that other thing round your neck!

Are   The cravat? Pox ma'am 'tis a disaster! Odious! My oaf of a man left it out and hid the rest.

Ann   Oh no it's a picture!

Are   Well insult me to my face. It but confirms that your tailor's bills are wasted on you. Pox ma'am, one of us must give up this damned foolish habit of followin' the fashion – and I'm damned sure it ain't me. I'll get something from the marriage!

Ann   Your lordship will tease.

Are   Tease ma'am! I never tease about fashion. On that subject I am always serious – and correct. Well today ye're pleased to ogle me like an ape, but ye commonly find my society tedious –

Ann (*aside*)   At last he's said something I agree with.

Are   – and as I never willingly discomfit a lady I'll relieve ye of it. I depart for London within the week to see to the refurbishments ordered to my house to console me at the time of my wedding. I told the designer the dining room should be apple green. He hath sent me a sample. If any apple were ever that colour Adam would not have been tempted and mankind would not have fallen.

Ann   O lawd sir why wait a week? I'll pack my things and we may be off –

Are   'Twas agreed ye spent six months in the country learning manners. A wholely optimistic time, but a newly married man is fond and believes in miracles – as well he may. Six months. 'Tis not my fault the designer hath gone colour-blind in one. Ye stay.

Ann   But sir how I can learn manners here? What refinement can I get from a duckpond?

Are   Try the parson's sister. But keep her off Deuteronomy. She once went to Bath. The visit was brief but she heard a concerto. She will hum ye the tune if ye ask her – and indeed, I believe, if ye do not.

Ann   Oh you pig! Pig!

Ann *throws a book at him. He picks it up.*

Are *(reads)*   *'The Duchess of Winchelsea's Guide to Conduct with Notes on Presentation at Court and Selected Subjects for Polite Conversation with Examples of Repartee, Condolence and so forth.'* I see ye have read it. Winchelsea is an illiterate hag whose conduct would have expelled her from a madhouse. Repartee? No one talks to her but Lord Lester and his repartee is as sparkling as a judge passing sentence of death. Ho! ye have much to learn.

Ann   I'll learn you this my lad! Your title lasted six hundred years but it'll likely die with you! I shan't enter your bedroom till you can hear the singing at Covent Garden when the window's shut!

Are   Fie ma'am! I intend to bequeath posterity the memorial of my life not some snot-nosed brat! If I have a boot or cape named after me – as I hope to have a hat – I shall be content.

Ann   You monster! You promised me –

Are   Ma'am a gentleman will promise anything to avoid quarrelling in church with a parson.

Ann   Not his vows you ape! My vows! You promised me
theatres, parties, dining in palaces, footmen, clothes. I was to
meet the prince. I didn't expect you to keep all your promises.
But you haven't kept one!

Are   Why ma'am if a gentleman kept his promises society
would fall apart. I promised. Forsooth and is that not enough?
Have ye not had the pleasure of the promise? Your feet tapped
when I promised you the opera! Your mouth watered when I
promised you diamonds! Your knees shivered when I promised
you the prince! What happiness I gave you! I denied you
nothing. I was a prodigal of promise. I promise all the time
I am a Christian. I go about the world scattering promises on
the suffering and destitute. Would ye have me hard-hearted
and not promise my fellow man in his misery? Fwaw! Be silent
ma'am! I promised! Ungrateful gal was that not enough but
that now you must have the promises kept? 'Tis plain folly in
a gentleman to keep his word. I verily believe that is the cause
of half the world's miseries. What surer way have we to drive
our friends to despair? I shall not be so cruel to any man that
it can ever be said I kept one promise I made him. Why, I
promise ye the stars! The Atlantic Ocean! There is no limit
to my generosity! I promise ye the moon! Now ma'am must
I keep my promise? Do ye not know that every man who ever
sighed has promised the moon to someone? Will ye all go
a-squabbling for it? Ma'am I wonder that ye can live in this
world at all with a mind so unschooled in polite society. The
sundial is promised the sun – yet is content to read the shadows!
I shall now promise to pay your tailor and if he hath wit enough
to thread a needle he'll know what that promise is worth.

Are *goes.*

Ann *(calls)*   Rose! O I have a new purpose to go to London.
Revenge. I'll shame him at the greatest soirée of the season. I'll
wait till the prince, to further his cause with me, is about to
offer him some high office and then say in a whisper loud
enough to wake the postilions in the street 'Nay sire, make him
an admiral and your chance of a liaison is gone' then sit back
and watch him cry in some magnificent palace.

Rose *comes in.*

Ann   Can you do voodoo?

Rose   Voodoo?

Ann (*indicating a jewel*)   I'll give you my pin.

Rose   No ma'am.

Ann   O you heartless brazen liar! It comes naturally to you people. You cut a chicken's neck and say spells.

Rose   I don't believe in that.

Ann   I don't have to keep you on when I get to London. Black girls aren't the novelty they were Miss Will-when-she-wants-to. You're two a penny. Listen Rose, this house is haunted. A girl was bricked up for carrying on out of wedlock. She comes out of the wall and wails. Dress up as the ghost and threaten my husband.

Rose   Bob wouldn't let me.

Ann   We shan't tell him.

Rose   If his lordship found out he'd sack both of us.

Ann   Very well. You had your warning. *I'll* do it!

DREAM (**Rose**)

I sit in a boat and float down a river of fire
The boat is cool – it doesn't burn in the heat
The flames hide us from the banks
Where the white man aims his gun
The boat sails safely on
The white men rage and stamp their feet
Then the fire flows up the banks and into the trees
The white men run and the fire comes out
The river of fir chases them till they fall
To their knees and crawl about in the flames
The river burns everything that stands in its path
Forests and men are all consumed in its wrath
   I am black
    At night I pass through the land unseen

Though you lie awake
    My smile is as sharp as the blade in my hand
But when the fire is spent
The ground is not scorched
The trees are not charred
The land is green in the morning dew
The cattle passed through the flames yet are not dead
Only the whiteman's bones are black
Lying by his burned-out tanks
Now cattle graze the river banks
Men and women work in the fields
All that they grow they own
To be shared by old and young
In the evening they rest
And the song of freedom is sung
    I am black
    At night I pass through the land unseen
    Though you lie awake
    My smile is as sharp as the blade in my hand
    The venom does not kill the snake

Scene Four

Hilgay. The Hall. 'The Thieving Scene.'

Workroom. Chest and chairs.

Mother *and* **Rose**. **Mother** *cleans silver and* **Rose** *sews.*

Mother   Ont lose things. Thass took. Knife an' fork. Be the
devil to pay. Yoo can write in my Loss Book so I ont hev to
bother parson.

Frank *comes in dazed, exhausted and filthy.*

Mother   Mornin' 'outside'. Don't mess in here, nough
t' clean up.

Frank   Bloody hole! In London yer work all hours but yer
not an animal. What am I here? Muck out the yard. Heave pig

shit. Ashamed t' smell meself. If I got back to London I wouldn't get a job in this state. Never wash the muck off me hands. Like bein' branded! Night-time I'm wore out. Creep into bed. If I had a bird I'd fall asleep on her. Fat chance of that! (*Without humour.*) Their fellas guard 'em with pitchforks. O Rosie I'm so tired I could cry. Why did we ever leave London?

Rose (*cradles* **Frank**'s *head*)   Hush.

He instantly falls asleep.

Mother   Yoo London folks are a proper laugh.

Rose   He's not used to workin' in the yard.

Mother   Git used, same's everyone else.

Rose   He don't mind working with his hands but that's *all* he does now. Likes to use his brains. He's smart – aren't you Frank? (*Shakes him awake.*)

Frank (*as if waking from a dream*)   Hens cacklin'. Cows roarin'. Horses kickin'. Dogs snarlin'. Bloody great mastiffs 'd rip yer hand off. Me nerves are in shreds.

Rose   Sit down.

Frank (*sits in* **Rose**'s *chair*)   Ta Rose. Yer a saint.

WOOD SONG (**Mother**)

The wooden cradle the wooden spoon
The wooden table the wooden bed
The wooden house the wooden beam
The wooden pulpit the wooden bench
The wooden hammer the wooden stair
The wooden gallows the wooden box
The iron chain the brass locks
The human toil the earthly span
These are the lot of everyman
The winds that drive the storms that blast
For everyman the die is cast
　　All you who would resist your fate
　　Strike now it is already late

Mother   My family polished this silver so long the pattern's
rub off. Mother say 'Fruits pluck and birds flown.' Her mother
an' her mother polished 'em in the winder to git the best light.
Howd 'em up an' see the colour of your eyes in 'em – then
they're clean. Show the babbys their face upside down in the
spoon, turn it round an' they're the right way up: one of the
wonders of the world. Kip 'em quiet for hours. Saw my face in
that when I were a kid. Mother say 'When yoor turn come,
yoo clean 'em as good as that, gal.' She's bin in the churchyard
twenty years. Wash 'em an' set 'em an' clean 'em after but ont
eat off 'em once. Food taste jist as good off mine.

Bob *comes in.*

Bob   Parson's called.

Mother   Goo upstairs?

Bob   Yip. Says a prayer – an' then off up to see her ladyship.

Mother   Git his glass of wine out on the hall table. Allus set
it ready. Old man his age need summat t' set him up.

Mother *goes out.*

Bob   Look at that lazy sod.

Takes some tape from the work basket and begins to tie **Frank** *to the
chair at the ankles, knees and elbows.*

Rose   What's that for?

Bob   Teach the lazy pig to sit.

Rose   He's wore out. (*Helps* **Bob** *with the tying.*) Go easy. I have
to account for every inch of that.

Bob   'He's wore out.' So 'm I dooin' his work. Truss up
lovely me old darlin'. There! Bet he's hevin' all sorts of dreams.
Ont know whass in store.

Frank *wakes and immediately opens his eyes.*

Frank   Bob. Undo me.

Bob   Ont fill the horse trough.

Frank Did. Buggers drunk it to cause a ruck. I'll fill it up again. Come on, don't get us into trouble.

Mother *comes in.*

Mother There. Thass set on the table with the saucer on top. Keep the flies out.

Frank (*trying to stand*) Come on Bob. It's no joke.

Bob (*tickling*) Ickle-wickle piggy goo to market. Ickle-wickle piggy stay at home. This ickle piggy goo wee-wee-wee!

Frank Git off! Bloody lunatic! Don't muck abaht.

Mother Spoon gone.

Rose Can't have. Count 'em.

Mother Can't count. Tell it's gone by the pattern. Knife, fork – where's the spoon? Who's bin in?

Frank Well I'm clear. I was tied up and fast asleep.

Mother Bob yoo ont got it?

Bob No.

Mother Rose? Hev to ask. It's my job. Easy git swep off by yoor skirt. Look in the pocket.

Rose Don't be daft.

Mother Look.

Rose (*looks*) No.

Frank (*wriggles*) This is bloody stupid. Parson nipped in on his way up. (*Stands.*) Rose get this off.

Mother Turn his pockets out.

Frank Now wait a minute! How could I do it? Truss up like a chicken.

Mother Could hev took it afore.

Frank (*jerks*) Now look here! Don't accuse me Mrs Hedges. Yer didn't use that tone to them.

Mother   I know they ont took it –

Frank   O do yer!

Mother   – and I'm me own judge a character. I lose my silver I lose my job. Ont git another one with a bad name.

Frank   Look son – get this bloody chair off or I'll break every bone in yer –

Bob   All right I believe yoo: yoo ont took it.

Frank   Ta. Now undo these bloody –

Bob   So we'll jist look in yoor pockets to satisfy Ma.

Frank (*tries hitting the chair on the floor*)   This has bloody well gone –

Rose   Let him go!

Rose *tries to untie* **Frank**. **Bob** *moves her aside*.

Bob   I'll settle this Rose.

Frank   Keep off son! I warn yer! Treat me like an animal, I'll be one!

Mother   Grab him Bob! He ont got the strength to hurt a fly!

Bob   Us'll hev to see Frank.

Frank   Look I didn't take it – an' what if I had? I get paid bugger all. Why? 'Cause in London I get tips. All yer pick up here's the shit on yer boots!

Bob *tries to search* **Frank**. **Frank** *spins and tries to defend himself with the chair legs*. **Bob** *and* **Frank** *fight*.

Bob   Quick Mum.

He grabs the chair and forces **Frank** *to sit.* **Frank** *struggles and jerks.*

Bob   Ont help boy: truss up like a rabbit.

Mother *tries to search* **Frank**.

Mother   Howd him steady! He's gooin' like –

Frank   Bitch! I'll kick yer bloody – smash yer bloody –

Mother   Beast! Beast! Beast!

Rose   Stop it! All of yer! Yer like kids.

Rose *starts to untie* **Frank***. She releases his arm. He takes the spoon from his pocket and holds it out.*

Frank   I hope it chokes yer.

Mother (*takes the spoon*)   Any damage t' that chair make it worse.

Frank *begins to untie himself.* **Rose** *helps him. Suddenly* **Bob** *turns the chair upside down.* **Frank***'s feet are in the air and his head is on the ground.* **Bob** *jerks the chair.*

Bob   Where yoo hid the rest?

Frank   That's the lot. Crowd round here it's a wonder there's anythin' left to nick.

Bob *lets the chair fall flat on its back on the floor.* **Frank** *again begins to untie himself.*

Bob   I'll search his loft.

Mother   I'll tell his lordship we've bin thief-catchin'. Parson's happen lucky, so I ont hev to send out for a magistrate.

Frank   Hold on. Yer got the spoon. That's the end of it.

Mother   Us'll tell boy.

Rose   Don't be daft Mother. There's no harm done. Frank'll go and get the knife an' fork – (*To* **Frank**.) an' everythin' else yer took – (*To* **Mother**.) an' yer can put it back. (*To* **Bob**.) Yer ruined my tape. Who's paying for that?

Frank   It's just the knife an' fork – God's honest.

Bob   Us'll hev to tell.

Rose   What's the good of that?

Bob   Ten't a question of good. Question of law. Ont break it us-self, an' if someone else do: we stay on the right side an' tell. 'S only way.

Mother   Fine Christian I'd be turnin' him loose on my neighbours. He'd hev t'steal to live on the road.

Frank   Yer have to steal in my job if yer wanna live. Yer fetch an' carry for 'em, pick 'em up, get 'em upstairs, put 'em to bed, clean up the spew. Stands to reason they drop anythin' – it's yourn. Give it back, they'd drop it again or lose it gamblin'.

Rose   For chrissake, Bob. They hang yer for stealin'.

Frank   Gawd.

Mother   If he was hungry I'd hev understand.

Frank   Look forget it an' I'll scarper. Yer'll never see me ugly mug again. Now that's somethin' to look forward to eh? No hard feelings. (*Finishes untying himself, stands and offers his hand.*) Say cheerio Ma? (*No response. Offers his hand to* **Bob**.) Come on old son. Don't upset Rose.

Bob   Ont trust yoo to goo through the gate: you'd nick it.

Frank   Gawd you peasants drive a hard bargain. Stickin' pigs, twistin' necks, carvin' balls off calves – no wonder they treat people like animals. (*To* **Rose**.) They after a cut? How much?

Rose (*to* **Bob**)   That lot can afford a bit of silver.

Mother   Can't Rose, only do us a disservice.

Rose   Please.

Bob   Yoo ont understand. I hev to take care of yoo now as well as Ma.

Frank   Gawd gal yer married a right little hypocrite there. Nasty little punk. Arse-crawlin' little shit –

Bob   Thass enough of that afore my mother.

He struggles with **Frank**. **Mother** *opens the lid of the chest and* **Frank** *is bundled in.* **Bob** *closes and bolts the lid.*

Bob   Soon settled his hash.

Frank (*inside*)   It's a madhouse!

Bob   You stay quiet an' think up a good excuse.

Mother   Phew he git me hot!

Frank *starts to kick and punch inside the chest.*

Mother   Ont yoo harm that chest boy! He's a proper vandal!

Bob (*aims a kick at the chest*)   That ont help. Doo yourself a mischief!

Frank (*inside*)   Rotten bastards!

Bob (*to* **Mother**)   Git parson an I'll git the rope. Rose yoo wait outside, ont stay an' be contaminated by his filth.

Frank (*inside*)   Filthy rotten swine! Shit. Rotten sod. God rot yer yer bastard!

Bob, **Mother** *and* **Rose** *go.* **Frank** *rattles the lid, trying to shake it open. Then he tries to knock off the end of the chest by kicking at it violently with both feet together.*

Frank (*inside*)   O Gawd they'll hang me. (*Thump.*) Please. Why did I come to this madhouse? (*Thump.*) Please Bob. Bastard. (*Thump.*) Can't stand bein' shut up! Go off me head! (*Violent shower of footfalls on the end of the chest.*)

Rose *has come in slowly. She stands and watches the chest.*

Frank (*inside*)   Can't breathe! I'll die! (*Shakes the lid with his hands, then tramples his feet on the end of the chest.*) Never do it again pal. I learned my lesson. O please Bob.

Kicking and struggling, changing to regular thumping, and all the while he groans. **Rose** *goes to the chest and gently sits on it. Immediately* **Frank** *is still.*

Frank (*inside*)   Bob? The spoon fell on the floor an' I was tempted. Honest. I know it's wrong but I – No no, it's dark Bob, I'm confused. Listen. I'll tell the truth. I took it to get me own back see? You 'ad yer head down tyin' me feet. I winked at Rose. She'll tell yer. O dear Bob yer fell for a trick there. We're gonna laugh. Come on old sport.

Rose   Frank. Listen carefully. Yer life depends on it.

Frank (*inside*)   O bless yer –

Rose   Hide in the yard in the little barn till it's dark. Then go. Stay off the road an' keep to the hedges. Yer –

Frank (*inside*)   No I'll scarper as fast as I –

Rose   If yer go on the road yer'll git caught. Where's the knife an' fork?

Frank (*inside*)   Rose what if they search the – . I promise.

Rose *stands and unbolts the chest.* **Frank** *opens the lid and steps out.*

Frank   Yer darlin'!

Rose   I'll get the stuff from yer loft.

Frank   Keep it angel! I'll help meself!

Frank *grabs the rest of the silver, drops some, grabs it again but still leaves a few pieces.*

Rose *watches him.*

Rose   O Frank.

Frank *runs out.* **Rose** *shuts the chest, bolts it and sits on it.* **Bob** *comes in with a heavy rope. He goes to the chest and* **Rose** *stands.*

Bob (*bangs lid with the flat of his hand*)   Gooin' to open yoor lid Frank. Yoo let me tie yoo up. No language – parson'll think thass Hebrew an' hev to look it up. Now then, git ready. (*Opens the lid.*) Ont git far.

Rose   Yer like a stranger.

Bob   Seems hard but it's for the best. Meddle in somethin' like this ruin yoor whole life. We think of us, can't afford to think of no one else. He took the risk, now he hev to pay. Ont no way out of that.

SONG OF THE CALF (**Bob**)

You take the calf to the slaughtering shed
It smells the sweat and blood and shit

It breaks its halter and runs through the lanes
The hollering men run after it

It snorts in the fresh clean morning air
It bellows and lows and tosses its head
And after it with sticks and ropes
Come the hollering men from the slaughtering shed

It reaches the town and runs through the streets
It tries to hide but the children shout
It turns at bay and trembles and groans
The hollering children have found it out

It scatters the mob and flees the town
It stops to rest in a quiet lane
Then peacefully strolls back home to its field
And enters the wooden gate again

And there stand the men from the slaughtering shed
In a circle with sticks and a halter and chain
They seize the calf and fetter it fast
And lead it back to the butcher again

For though it run and bellow and roar
The calf will be tied to the slaughterhouse door
The butcher will cut its throat with his knife
It will sink to its knees and bleed out its life

The morning is over, the work is done
You eat and drink and have your fun
The butcher is sharpening his knife today
Do you know – do you care – who will get away?

Bob   Best git started.

Rose (*points*)   He helped himself again.

Bob (*stares*)   Rose yoo git us into terrible trouble.

Rose   If yer catch him he'll tell – anythin' to get back at you.
Let's hope he gets away.

Bob   Well thass a rum un! I come to tie up a thief an I hev to
help him git off! (*Tugs the rope between his hands in bewilderment and
frustration.*)

Rose   He's hiding in the yard in the little barn. I'll take him some grub later on. Me mother told me what the slaves do when they run. The owners go tearin' down the road, even the dogs – glad to be off the chain. Me mother said stay quiet an' wait for the chance: it'll come.

Bob   Rose, yoo scare me. Ont talk like that, ont even think it. You're one of us now, yoo hev to think like white folk. (*Quietly.*) Yoo're a soft gal Rose, too easy touched: thass a canker.

Rose   I won't do things I grew up to hate.

Bob (*holds her*)   Wish I ont married if thass only gooin' to bring this sort of trouble. O Rose, Rose . . .

Parson *comes in.*

Bob   Beg pardon Parson, wife's upset . . . He's gone.

Parson   Dear me.

Bob   Ont set the bolt proper. My fault. (*Steps away from* **Rose**.)

Parson   Bob you cost your master. Get after him. Take every horse and man from the fields. We have taken a viper to our bosom. (*To* **Mother** *as she comes in.*) Did I spy my glass of Madeira under its friendly blue saucer? If you would be so kind. The excitement has parched my throat. Bob, scour every road.

Bob   He took the rest of the silver.

Mother (*stares*)   O the wicked man! (*Bursts into tears.*) My silver gone! The wicked man! Wicked! (*She weeps and sobs the word 'wicked' as she kneels and collects the remaining silver from the floor.*)

Parson   There: see how the guilty afflict the innocent. This woman learns of a lifetime's wasted labour. The cherished things on which she lavished her affection are gone. How will she occupy the time she would have devoted to cleaning them? And who is to say that in the hotness of pursuit fear has not triumphed over greed? Even now the loot may lie in the mud at the bottom of a ditch.

Mother (*weeping*)   O Parson don't say so!

Parson   Or be hurled down a well, lost for ever!

Mother   Whatever shall us do?

Bob   I'll take the men right out to the coach road. He'll make for there.

Parson   Ten commandments! That's all that are asked of us. One little law for each finger, to bring peace to the lord in his palace and the goodman in his cottage. Yet ten are too many. They live by one: self − and seek perdition. (*To* **Rose**.) O you mustn't think all Englishmen are rogues my dear. I assure you most are as upright and sensible as your dear husband. Well, I'll fetch the Madeira. (*He goes.*)

MAN GROANS (**Rose** *and* **Mother**)

The house is on fire
Dark figures wave from the roof!
Shall we fetch a ladder
Or light brands to burn down the rest of the street?

You to whom the answer is easy
Do not live in our time
You have not visited our city
You weep before you know who to pity
Here a good deed may be a crime
And a wrong be right
To you who go in darkness we say
It's not easy to know the light

A man sits hunched in a cell
People dance in the street
Shall we stretch our hands through the bars
Or run to the street and dance in triumph?

You to whom *etc.*

A man groans in a ditch
We take off our coat
To cover the man in the ditch
Or give to the man who runs away?

You to whom *etc.*

Scene Five

Hilgay. The Hall. Breakfast room.

Table set for breakfast. Two chairs.

Are *reads a London newspaper.*

Are   When I go to the city of light Hedges stays her in outer darkness. Because my forebears had the lice combed from their beards by yokels must I have my cravat ruined by one? I shall –

Stops short at what he reads in the paper. **Ann** *comes in as a ghost.*

Are   That damned little Lordling Lester! The ninth time he's squirted into print since my departure! Plague rot his little ermined soul! I'll rout that martinet at his capers and see –

He sees the ghost.

Why I'll put on last year's breeches! The family ghost! (*Puts down the paper.*)

Ann   Woe!

Are   Be off with ye! Disturbin' a gentleman at his breakfast! (*Picks up his newspaper and shoos it.*) Shoo I say!

Ann   Hear me Lord Are!

Are   Hear ye! What listen to an ague-ridden corpse! When I want news or advice I'll go to someone a damned sight livelier than thou art ma'am. When were you last at court or the play? Ye gad! what d'ye know of fashion? I'll wear something a sight more sprightly to be buried in! It amazeth me ye are not ashamed to be seen so in modern times!

Ann   Thy poor wife!

Are   My wife! What of my wife? (*Aside.*) Here's a to-do, discussin' me wife with a ghost – though the subject is fitting. Have ye come to tell me she's to join ye? I thank ye for the good news and bid ye be gone so I may celebrate in peace!

Ann (*aside*)   The monster! – Thy wife must flee to London. Flee!

Are   To London? Why?

Ann   She is with child. If 'tis born here 'tis for ever cursed.

Are   Forsooth? And who will bear the expense of a London lying in? Let the cow-doctor child her, as he did all my family. A curse? Lawd 'twill curse me for cursing it with its mother! But 'tis to be hoped it's a sensible brat and will understand it was the she-cat or poverty – and his poor papa made the best of the bad bargain.

Ann (*aside*)   O my London revenge! I'll smear the paint on his face in the royal presence! – Alas that noble woman!

Are   If ye pity her go and keep her company. I am not so hard put that I must seek the society of a ghost. I tell ye this spirit: I had thought to have been too harsh with the slut, but if it's with brat I'm off tomorrow. Her morning sickness will be nauseous.

Ann (*aside*)   I'll frighten the monster to death!

Ann *goes.*

Are (*muttering to himself as he settles at the table and resumes his newspaper*)   Damned impertinent she-spirit, to disturb a man outside calling hours. I see the editorial doth not advise us the ghosts are walking. 'Tis a good story – yet I cannot use it. I'd have the Methodists roaring hymns at my door and asking to see my spirit. Still, the news gives a man relish to his breakfast. London! Blessed city! Our New Jerusalem! Soon my shadow shall fall on thy doorways, my sprightly foot ascend thy broad stairs, my melodious voice sound in thy tapestried halls. London London London thou art all! I thank thee spirit and shall drink thy health when I come to town.

Ann *comes in.*

Ann   Woe! Woe!

Are   'Tis intolerable! Have ye come to tell me the news was mistaken?

Ann   Thy poor wife. That dearest, loveliest creature, that paragon of –

Are   Pox! If thy news is so great it brings thee from the grave twice then tell it!

Ann   If thy wife goes not to London thy wealth is lost!

Are   This is arrant posturing! She hath raised thee to badger me. She stays. Go! I defy thee. (*Aside.*) 'Fore God I am taken with my style. Who'd have thought I'd unloose such a show of bravado?

Ann   Thy wife –

Are   Stays.

Ann   Then curses on your ugly face! Your evil old –

Are   I shall not have my face insulted at breakfast by a zombie!

Are *goes.*

Ann   O the wretch! I'll poison him! No I'll poison myself and haunt him!

Are *comes back with a drawn rapier.*

Are   Out, vapour! (*Whirls his rapier.*) I shall stir you up and blow you off in a mist!

Ann   O wretch!

Are   It backs! What – ye remember cold steel? Have at ye! I would not be inhospitable to anyone but ye have a place: the wall – or anywhere at all of Lord Lester's. A man may breakfast at peace in his home before he's reminded there is religion – or it's not England.

Are *runs* **Ann** *through.*

Ann   O. (*Falls.*)

Are   Why, 'tis a heavy ghost! I had thought to go whisk-whisk and – as I am a gentleman – opened the window for it and it had vanished in a puff of smoke. The ghost bleeds. (*Stoops, examines.*) 'Fore God 'tis flesh and blood. My wife. (*Steps back. His voice falls and he presses the index finger to the side of his mouth.*)

Hssssssssssss . . . here's a fine how-d'ye-do. My wife. Stretched
out on the floor. With a hole in her breast. Before breakfast.
How is a man to put a good face on that? An amendment
is called for. It were a foolish figure I should cut. A buffoon.
Murdered his wife. Got up like a ghost. Before breakfast.
I break into cold sweat when I think of how I should use it
had it befallen Lord Lester. I could not put my foot in a duke's
door again. Never ascend the stairs to a hall blazing with
chandeliers. Or ogle the ladies from the *balcon réservé* of a pump
room. My life would be over. (*Nibbles toast.*) Cold. Faw! (*Puts
toast down.*) A fine kettle of fish! (*Rings.*) Well you'd best sit at
your husband's table. Hopefully 'twill look as if our quarrel
had been less violent. Stretched out on the floor can only
encourage the lowest surmise. (*Sets* **Ann** *in a chair.*) A man
cannot think with his dead wife sprawled on the carpet. And
I must think – after I've tired my brains with choosing a suit
for the day.

Bob *comes in.*

Are   Toast. This is as cold as a corpse – yea, and as hard as a
tombstone.

Bob   That be all my lord?

Are   For the moment.

Bob   Right my lord.

He takes the toast rack from the table and goes.

Are   O thou Great Boob. Thou art my deliverer. Thou
mayest be relied on. Thou art a loon and shall serve. (*Adjusts*
Ann.) To arrange thee better. Faith thy silence is wonderful!
Hadst thou behaved so when thou livst thou mightst have lived
longer. Thy costume becomes thee. At last thy tailor hath done
thee justice. Thy face had always a lowering look. You play
death to the life. A performance to retire on.

Are *goes.* **Bob** *comes in with toast in a silver rack, goes to the table and
steals a cup of coffee. He sees* **Ann**. *He drops the toast.*

Bob   Eek! Lawd defend us! The dead are risen!

Are *comes back.*

Are   What man?

Bob (*points*)   Th – th – th –

Are   Ye have burned the toast? Twice in one morning!

Bob   No' – th' – no' – th' –

Are   Is the child possessed?

Bob   Th' – *there*!

Are (*goes to the chair and looks at* **Ann**)   There is a ghost.
O Robert thou art possessed! What have ye done?

Bob   Eek! A ghost!

Are   How it spies at thee! It comes for thee Robert.

Bob (*sinks to his knees*)   O no am I goin' to die? O lawd defend
us!

Are   What venom! Shut thine eyes Bob lest it ensnare thee.

Bob (*shuts his eyes*)   Ah! Eek! Oo!

Are   Take the rapier.

Bob   The – ?

Are   Beside thee. (*He kicks the rapier along floor.*) Hold the handle
for a cross.

Bob   Lawd! Lawd! (*One arm across his eyes, the rapier held out in
the other hand.*) Mercy! Save us!

Are *lifts* **Ann** *from behind.*

Are   Robert! Robert! Take care! It advanceth at thee!

Bob (*peeps from under his arm*)   Ah! O!

Are *manipulates* **Ann**.

Are   I struggle with it. It tears itself towards thee. God what
strength! It will have ye!

Bob   No! No! No! No!

Terror! **Are** *makes ghost sounds and lifts* **Ann** *towards* **Bob**. **Bob**
points the rapier. **Are** *leans* **Ann** *on the rapier's point.*

Are   O Robert. Open your eyes.

Bob (*eyes covered*)   Hev it gone? (*Uncovers eyes.*)

Are   See! the ghost – the rapier – you: joined. Bob what have
ye done?

He pushes **Ann** *with a finger: she topples.*

Are   Murdered your mistress.

Bob   My mistress?

Are   'Tis – 'twas – she. I cannot say why she is so dressed.
I do not recall she mentioned a fancy-dress breakfast. It seems
unlikely. Who can fathom the mind of one suddenly raised to
the peerage? Did she suppose society breakfasted in this
extravagant fashion? We can never know. Impetuous Bob, how
often have I warned ye?

Bob   Impetuous?

Are   Certainly. Ye have murdered your mistress. Before
breakfast. What greater proof of impetuosity?

Bob   But I – took it for a ghost!

Are   As I say: impetuous Bob. I struggled with ye, but thou
art a robust fellow and overcame me – and then, I had not
breakfasted.

Bob   What have I done?

Are   Murdered your mistress. Before breakfast. Pray do not
stand there with your rapier dripping blood on my carpet.
Hand it to me – (*Takes the rapier.*) lest ye turn it against me –

Bob   Never my lord!

Are   – in your present rashness. In one of your sudden fits.
I see it now. A practical joke, a jape. Her ladyship ennuied by
rural life – which must be said in her favour – tried thus to
brighten our morning. But Bob you have no sense of humour.

Bob   No sir. I just do my job.

Are   This morning you were overzealous. Pick up the toast.

Bob (*picking up the toast*)   What's to be done sir?

Are   The future rests with the authorities – as it always does. (*Looks at a piece of toast.*)   Blood. I shall not breakfast this morning. Forget the toast. One shudders at what you would do on your third attempt to bring it.

Bob   I begin to see what I hev done: I hev widowed my master.

Are   Before breakfast. Few can say as much. I shall miss her pranks – this is presumably the last. Bob was I ever a bad master?

Bob   Thass what makes it worse! Her poor ladyship.

Are   Well she was not altogether without blame. Never play jokes on the servants. It agitates them into dropping things. That at least we have learned this morning. (*Rings.*)

Bob   What yoo dooin'?

Are   We have a difficult road ahead. Turn to me at all times. I shall lead ye to the promised land. Hold no conferences with others, who will mislead you.

Bob   Yes sir. I've made my mistake once. O thank yoo sir.

Are   Do not fumble my hand Bob. Ye have slain my wife and I have completed my toilet.

Mother *comes to the door.*

Are   Mrs Hedges her ladyship is dead.

Mother   Beg pardin' sir?

Are   Her ladyship is dead.

Mother   Dead?

Are (*aside*)   O the tedium of a tragedy: everything is said twice and then thrice.

Mother (*flatly*) Dead?

Are (*aside*) Twice.

Mother (*flatly*) Dead!

Bob Dead!

Are (*aside*) I have survived the morning tolerably well, now I shall spoil it with a headache.

Mother (*suddenly realising*) Her ladyship is dead!

Are (*aside*) If she is not she is a consummate actress.

Mother Is her ladyship dead?

Are (*aside*) O God is it to be put to the question? We shall have pamphlets issued on it. There are really no grounds for this aspersion on my swordsmanship.

Mother Ah! Er! O! (*Weeps.*)

Are (*aside*) Now the wailing and hallooing. Lungs of leather from coursing their dogs, throats like organ pipes from roaring their hymns. Well I have an immaculate excuse for retiring to my room, and as it cannot return I shall use it. – Mrs Hedges if ye have no pan on the fire pray run to the magistrate and tell him Bob has murdered his mistress. Before breakfast.

Mother Eek! Murdered? Bob?

Bob Alas!

Are (*aside*) And now the convulsions they learn at country dancing. – Mind, not parson Mrs Hedges. Captain Sludge. I could not endure parson's consolations on an empty stomach. (Bob throw the toast to the hens on your way to prison.)

Bob, *weeping, picks up the toast rack and nods.*

Are I shall have to contend with parson at the graveside. Sludge is a plain bluff man who made many fields sanguinary with the blood of his sovereign's foes. He won't set the windows rattling at the sight of one dead woman. Mrs Hedges to Captain Sludge.

Bob   Ought to give her ladyship a sheet. Ont decent lyin'
there. (**Bob** *and* **Mother** *wail.*) Captain's is too far for Mother
in her state of aggravation. I'll hand meself in.

Are   'Tis handsome Bob, but I cannot let a murderer wander
the fields. Superstition is rife: the hands would refuse to
harvest. – Mrs Hedges the chimney tops will rattle down
scattering fire and ash as if Hilgay were the sister city to
Gomorrah. Your wailing will start the dogs! Bob wait. I'll send
a man from the kennels. The dogs have been walked.

Are *goes.*

Bob   If it weren't for his lordship I'd kill meself.

Mother   Don't talk so daft. (*She hits him.*) Put a brave face on
it. Parson'll speak up for yoo if his lordship doo. Whole a
Hilgay'll rally round. Yoo ont step out a line afore – not till yoo
married. An yoo married her in London (*She hits him.*) so it ont
count. Why! if they had to find an ordinary chap they ont find
one more ordinary than yoo boy.

Part Two

Scene Six

Peterborough.

Gaol. Cell. Upstage door to another cell.

Rose *and* **Bob**. **Bob** *is shackled to the floor.*

Rose What happened?

Bob It'll be all right. (*He tries to comfort her but she walks away.*)

Rose What happened?

Bob Ont know. (*Shakes his head.*) 'S'n accident.

Rose They have accidents, we make mistakes.

Bob Rose I hev a worry. There were blood on her afore I stab her.

Are, **Parson** *and* **Gaoler** *come in.*

Are Robert you bear up bravely.

Bob Sir. Parson.

Parson Bless you. (*To* **Rose**.) Bless you child.

Are (*aside to* **Parson**) This is a sorry sight: my livery in a cell.

Are *tips the* **Gaoler**. *He goes.*

Bob We're jist tryin' to sort out what happened.

Are Bob Bob, why trouble your head with things that don't concern it?

Rose Her ladyship was bleedin before –

Are Like a loyal wife your head is in as great a whirl as your husband's. (*Aside.*) The turnkey shall forbid her the cell. 'Tis seemly in a hanging.

Frank (*off*)   Pleasure brought me to my end! What brought you, yer cantin' hypocrite?

Are (*to* **Parson**)   My former footman. When we're finished here I'll go and rattle my cane through his bars.

Bob (*calls*)   Ont hang. His lordship stand by me.

Frank (*off*)   Trust that fox an' yer deserve t' hang! Yer no friend of mine Bob Hedges but I don't wish him on yer!

Are   Mr Phelps next door.

Parson   My lord?

Are   We cannot let that fellow die with his soul in such neglect. For charity, go to him.

Parson   Your lordship is a wonder! Even now I was silently praying I might be asked.

Parson *goes out to fetch the* **Gaoler**.

Are   Well miss?

Rose   My husband didn't kill her.

Bob (*quietly*)   Bless you Rose. Yoo're the brave one here.

Are   Bob –

Bob   She were bleedin' when I come in.

Are   Let me consider. (*Goes to one side.*) The sun rose on the horizon – and fell back, and all the world is darkness. Courage good heart. If the sun goes from its course, why – bring it back. The oaf will hang and the truth with him. But it must be done quietly, and now the hussy will drag me in. Lester will scrawl me up on the wall of every jakes as a jack-in-the-box with a sword in its hand! 'Tis intolerable.

He goes back to them.

Bob, I must tell thee plainly thou art a trouble and deserve thy wife: yet I wish ye the same happy deliverance I had. What you or I say is no matter. Truth is what the lawyers say it is. You have have none, whilst I . . . (*Gesture.*) If Bob confesses, the killing is an accident. If he accuses me – well, have ye ever listened dumbfounded while ye contradicted yourself ten times in a minute? My lawyers will torment him till he runs to the scaffold – many an innocent man has willingly hanged to be rid of a lawyer. What if I go into the dock? Would ye give evidence against me Bob? A lord dragged down by a working man? 'Tis against all civil order. Ye see the enormity of the thing? We are at the heart of the matter. In my person I am society, the figurehead of law and order. Make me a fool or a villain and the mob will dance in the street. If ye will be innocent Bob anarchy must triumph, your windows be broken, your mother's head cracked and your wife stoned for a blackamoor. (*He takes* **Bob** *aside. His chain rattles.*) Come, we are Englishmen and may talk freely together. Ye have this chance to serve your country. Robert the Hero, hail! The nation asks it of ye. Stand trial. Be acquitted. I'll buy the jury. I withdraw while ye consider your reply.

THE GENTLEMAN (**Bob** *and* **Rose**)

Who would raise a whip when an order is obeyed?
Why lift up your fist when a pointing finger will lead?
Who would raise their voice when soft words will do my friend?
Why use a knife when a smile makes cuts that bleed?
When you have the mind why bother to chop off the head?
When white hands will do the work why make your hands red?

The **Parson** *returns with the* **Gaoler**. *The* **Gaoler** *lets the* **Parson** *into the cell upstage. The* **Gaoler** *lounges beside the open door and waits.*

Rose   He's guilty.

Bob   Yes, but that ont seem to matter. We accuse him, we'll starve gal. Never git another job's long's we live. We jist hev to go along for the sake of appearance – like he say.

Rose   But he's guilty and you're –

Bob (*head in hands*)   Less think woman!

Frank (*off*)   Sold the silver and lived like a lord. Whored in the mornin', whored in the afternoon, whored in the evenin' when I weren't pissed.

Are (*calls*)   Confound it Parson, pray to some effect!

Frank (*off*)   He's on his knees doin' his best, aren't yer old cock?

The **Parson** *comes in.*

Parson   Patience sir. When they're to hang there's nothing to threaten them with. Not even hell. In this atheistical age they don't believe in it.

The **Parson** *goes back to the cell.*

Frank (*off*)   Swillin' an' screwin till the silver run out. Then I lived in the fields. Robbed the churches.

Parson (*off*)   'Tis not a confession, 'tis boasting.

Frank (*off*)   Jumped out the hedges onto the women and screwed 'em in the ditch! The last wild beast in England! I almost made London! Open winder in Barnet. Put me hand in. Son of the house knock me out. Drag back here. But it was worth it!

Are (*calls*)   Parson, muzzle him with your cassock. – Robert my business presses.

Bob   A minute longer.

Frank (*off*)   Oi! Is that Lord Arse?

Parson (*off*)   Purge his heart and still his tongue.

Parson *runs out of the cell.* **Gaoler** *slams the door and locks it.*

Frank (*appears at the grill in the door*)   Is that you Arsehole?

Bob (*to* **Rose**)   Least this way we got a chance.

Rose   I won't keep quiet.

Frank (*at grill*)   Arsehole! I can smell yer! I thought it was the prison sewer! God rot yer, yer pox-ridden rat!

Rose   If we don't speak now it'll be too late.

Frank (*at grill*)   Arsehole!

Are (*rattling his cane through the grill*)   Fellow if your insults had any wit I'd stay to applaud. (*To* **Bob**.) 'Tis a great sadness but I see ye will stand on your own.

Are goes to the door and is about to leave. **Bob** *gestures to him to wait.*

Frank (*at grill*)   Arsehole! I thought my life had no more pleasure! It's worth hanging to call you cur to your face!

Bob   It's according as your lordship wishes.

Are   Good – you choose your protector well.

Frank (*falls down*)   Rot yer!

Sounds of raving. **Gaoler** *opens the door of* **Frank**'s *cell.* **Parson** *goes in and almost immediately comes out to shout at* **Are**.

Parson   Beware! Your lordship's adjacency brings on convulsions. He crawls upon his stomach on the floor. He'll die before scaffolding day!

Are *goes.*

Bob (*to* **Rose**)   I played the sheep, now I'll play the man. I'll git us through. Ont fret Rose. I'd rather hev yoor smile.

Parson (*peers through the open doors of the cell at* **Frank**)   A serpent or a great newt!

Frank (*off*)   Rot! Rot! Rot him!

Parson (*running downstage*)   Gaoler! 'Tis from Revelations!

Frank *lurches into the cell. His hands are manacled. His leg chain pulls him short and he crashes to the floor.*

SONG OF TALKING (**Bob** *and* **Frank**)

> My mate was a hard case
> Worked beside me on the bench for years
> Hardly said a word
> Talking isn't easy

When the machines run
One day he dropped a coin
He unscrewed the safety rail to get it back
The press-hammer struck his head
He looked up at the roof and he said
   The green hills by the sea
   Where the light shines
   Through tall dark pines
A minute later he was dead

Didn't speak even on the street
Once I saw him shopping with his wife
He only nodded
He was decent to me
But I'd heard rumours
He'd done time in chokey
And his fist could hit you like a steel-capped boot
Then he unscrewed the safety rail
I nursed him on the concrete floor
He looked up at the roof and said
   The green hills by the sea
   In the dark grove
   I first made love
A minute later he was dead

My mates ran to fetch the nurse
The foreman wouldn't stop the machines
I bent to listen
He looked like an apprentice
He was gently crying
And babbling to himself
I touched his hand – no response
The hammer was still beating
I nursed him on the concrete floor
He looked up at the roof and said
   The green hills by the sea
   Through the tall dark trees
   The sea weaves
   A shining thread
A minute later he was dead

Scene Seven

Hilgay. The Hall. Workroom.

Mrs Hedges *peels potatoes.* **Rose** *comes in.*

Rose   They found 'im guilty.

Mother (*continues to peel potatoes*)   'Is lordship'll take care of it.

Rose   Are killed 'er.

Mother (*stops peeling in alarm*)   Howd yoor row, gal. Yoo'll git us all threw out on us necks. Hardache's come. Waitin' outside. Say yoo wrote 'im. Yoo let on what's gooin' on 'ere, I'll cuss the day you wed my Bob.

Rose   They'll 'ang 'im.

Mother   Ont talk so far back! No sense of proportion. This is 'is big chance. Doo 'is lordship a favour like this 'e's set up for life. (*Starts peeling potatoes again.*) Poor people can't afford t' waste a chance like this. God know it ont come often. Yoo start trouble, 'oo pay? Us. *Yoo're* back t' London, *we* git chuck out. End up in the work'ouse: work like a slave, work'ouse disease – ont last six month. Too old t' 'ave my life mess up. So ont meddle Rose.

Rose   Bob's in prison waitin' t' be –

Mother   Worse places outside. Ont' expect 'is lordship t' goo in the dock for the like of 'er. Jist drag the family name through the mire. Ont know where t' look next time I goo t' the village, they know I work for someone like that. Silly woman deserved t' git killed. She come into my kitchen dress up, I give 'er a whack a my fryin' pan she ont git up from. Jist ont stand in my boy's way when 'e hev 'is chance t' goo up in the world. 'Sides, even if what yoo say's true – which it ont – if my Bob stood up in court an' spoke *rashness* 'bout 'is lordship, 'ood believe 'im? If there's a row between man an' boss, stand t' reason 'oo win.

Rose   It ain' between man and boss. It's between two bosses.

Mother (*still peeling potatoes*)   Now whass she on about?

Rose   It pays t' know the law when you're black. No one can benefit from their own crime.

Mother *snorts in derision.*

Rose   If Are killed 'is wife, 'e loses 'er money.

Mother *stops peeling.*

Rose   It goes back to the next of kin: 'er father.

Hardache *comes in. He carries a walking stick and mops his face and neck.*

Hardache (*gesturing behind him*)   Pretty place. Sorry I missed the funeral. Carry on, Mrs – Hedges in't it?

Mother *starts to peel potatoes again.*

Hardache   A neighbour had to sell up and I couldn't miss the opportunity. Rose you married a villain, but no one's perfect.

Mother (*stops peeling potatoes*)   That wicked gal's got it in 'er 'ead my Bob ont do it.

Hardache   Not do it? Is that right, Rose? Then who did?

Rose   Are.

Hardache   His lordship? Nay, I've never 'eard the like. Happy young couple like that? Why ever should he be so rash? No no, she were struck down by your over-hasty young man. I can't believe otherwise.

Mother *starts to peel again.*

Hardache   His lordship you say? Well, I'm struck both ways sideways.

Mother *goes on peeling but watches* **Hardache** *intently.*

Hardache   What a predicament to fall into our laps – (*Quickly correcting himself.*) land on our heads. A real taremadiddle and no mistake. Did he strike her, Rose?

Rose Yes sir.

Hardache I shan't take kindly to bein' deceived, Mrs
Hedges. Now's the time to speak out. You know what's at
stake: my daughter's memory. D'you know owt?

Mother (*carefully peeling*) Well – I doo an' I don't. What
should I say?

Hardache The truth woman! It's a Christian country in't it?

Mother (*as before*) Well – if 'is lordship kill 'er – what's the
good of what I say?

Hardache What good? When I think of that innocent
young man – you did say he was innocent, Rose? – alone in his
cell, my withers weren't more wrung for me own daughter.
Well Mrs Hedges?

Mother I suppose – if that's 'ow it is – (*She stops peeling.*) I hev
t'tell Mr Hardache my son towd me 'e ont do it.

Hardache And also testified Are cajoled him into covering
up his own crime. What a dastardly villain!

Mother *finishes repeating his words in her attempt to memorise them.
The peeling knife and a potato are held up in the air over the bowl.*

Mother . . . coverin' up 'is own crimes what a dastardly
villain.

Hardache Well. Now we know. I'm right glad I came to pay
respects to my daughter's grave: you run into business anywhere.
(*To* **Rose**.) Leave all to me lass. Mind, no speakin' out of turn.
The fish still has to be landed by an expert tickler. Good day.

Rose Will you go straight to the judge?

Hardache Tch, tch, didn't I say leave all to me?

Rose I'll show you the stairs to the –

Hardache Nay, I can't be seen ascendin' from the servants'
quarters. Best slip out round to the front. Don't want to put
suspicion into his lordship's mind if e's' acquired the habit of
murder.

Hardache *goes out the way he came.*

Mother   Ont stand there, gal! Sit 'em on the stove. Dinner'll come 'round t'day jist as it did yesterday.

Rose *goes out with the bowl of peeled potatoes.*

IN AN ENGLISH COUNTRY LANE

In an English country lane
Larks trilled in the sky
Flowers danced in the corn
Roses twined round the door
I met a man with a sack on his back
And a staff in his hand
Like a pilgrim in days of yore
Set out for a foreign land
I never asked where he went or why
Or what his pack was for
As he passed I said good day my friend
And thought of him no more

In an English country lane
Larks screamed in the sky
Poppies danced like blood-red hands
And children hid in the door
I met a man with a pack on his back
And a city plan in his grasp
Like an invader in days of yore
I never asked why he carried a bomb
Or what his plan was for
Or where his journey would end
He looked straight ahead
As if he already lay with the dead
On the tube train's blood-red floor
And as he passed I said
Why are you my enemy my friend?

How can the hour of peace be struck
While children cower inside the door
And roses drip blood on the threshold stone?
The dead are always alone – let mercy have pity

Has the city given you all the bodies you need?
Or do you want more?
You set out but where will your journey end?
Why are you my enemy my friend?

Scene Eight

Peterborough. Holme Cottage. Kitchen. Table. Chairs.

Bob *and* **Parson**. **Bob***'s legs are fettered. He scratches a pen on paper.*

Bob   Hev a skill for learnin. Jist lack the opportunity afore.
Letters is a miracle Parson. Dance afore yoor eyes an goo
t'gither like a candle flarin up afore it die. Are say I'll be put
in charge of clerkin. Scribe his bills.

Parson   Bob do not set your heart on a pardon. Seek
salvation.

Bob   Ont be so glum Parson. For the moment us hev t' make
the best of a bad way.

Mrs Wilson *comes in.*

Mrs Wilson   Don't splash your ink on my ceiling. Your
mother's here. (*Gives* **Bob** *a duster.*) Wipe your manacles. Don't
want visitors thinking I don't keep you in a proper state. Look
at my floor!

Mrs Wilson *goes out.*

Bob (*annoyed as he puts down his pen and takes up the duster*)   Drat!
(*Polishing his chains.*) Look clean enough t' me. (*To* **Parson**.) 'S
natural yoo fret. Come now ol' friend, on't like t' see yoo so
depress. Cheer up an smile, doo us'll git cross.

Parson (*aside*)   The child's a simpleton. Lord Are promises a
pardon to comfort him and heaps coals of fire on his head.

Bob (*throws down duster*)   Done! (*Takes up pen.*) In t' battle!

Parson   Hedges put down that pen and listen! Our battle is
with Satan. Bob – have you heard?

Bob   Ay Parson, our battle with Satan. (*Aside as he puts down the pen.*) Us'll hev a sermon now.

Parson   What befell his lordship on that tragic morning – before breakfast – it is not my office to enquire. But his lordship is adamant t'was you. As God made water clear, you are surely innocent. But you must hang. It is your duty.

Mrs Wilson *comes in with a broom and sweeps round the feet of* **Bob** *and the* **Parson**.

Parson   Lord Are is the guardian of our laws and orderer of our ways. Topple him from his mighty seat and Beelzebub will walk the lanes of Hilgay. Already the Methodists rant at his lordship.

Bob (*trying to concentrate*)   . . . rant at his lordship.

Parson   Someone must hang.

Mrs Wilson (*to* **Bob**)   Up.

Bob *raises his feet and she sweeps under them.*

Parson   Then the village will return to its ancient peace and Satan be shut in that darkness which even his abominable fires cannot illuminate.

Mrs Wilson (*sweeping*)   Winter coming but no one helps me with the fuel bill.

Parson   In truth we are all sinners. He who walks on the water leaves no footprints for us to follow in.

Bob   . . . footprints for us t' follow in.

Parson   Be of good cheer! You are not the first man asked thus to die for his country – nor will you be the last. Bob! – pay attention.

Bob (*starts*)   Ay.

Parson   For now I must enter into theology.

Bob (*aside to* **Mrs Wilson**)   Take the kettle off Mrs Wilson. If he's in t' *that* us'll be late for tea.

Parson   Your summary demise will atone for Adam's sin in Hilgay.

Bob (*aside to* **Mrs Wilson**)   An' supper by the sound of it.

Parson   Purify thy heart! You cannot confess to murdering your mistress before breakfast – but you've lived long enough to assemble your own goodly collection of flaws! Repent! Soon you will go to the bosom of your lord. To enter that hallowed place you must be spotless – Mrs Wilson cannot follow after you with her broom.

Mrs Wilson   I need a new broom. They ought to be provided by the authorities.

Mrs Wilson *goes out.*

Parson   Bob have you followed what I've said?

Bob   Nope. Sorry, Parson. I give up listening weeks back. Jist 'cause a bloke's told he's t' hang everybody think they hev the right t' sermonise him. Jist leave me t' git my book. Then I can read my pardon. (*Reads.*) 'M-a-n-i-s-w-h-a-t-h-e-k-n-o-s-e.'

Parson   What?

Bob   Kernosy!

Parson   Knows! The 'k' is silent and the 'e' modulates! – how many more times! *Man is what he knows.*

Bob   Ask me the chap who invented writing ont know how t' spell.

Parson (*aside*)   Let us leave him to his book. If he go to heaven with a mind able to read he will show God he hath laboured in the vineyard to put some light into its natural darkness – though indeed this place is more like a tavern. (*Sighs. To* **Bob**.) Remember the silent 'k'!

Mother *comes in.*

Mother   Bob.

They do not embrace because she must put down her shopping.

Bob   Where's Rose?

Mother   Ont allowed in. She's outside. (*Shrugs.*) Would come.

Bob (*goes to door and calls*)   Rose! Rose!

Parson   I'll go to her. Remember Bob: the best behaviour as befits your state.

Bob   I want her here!

Parson *goes out.*

Mother   Well if thass all the welcome I git I may's well goo home. Thought it'd've all blow over by now. Hev yoo back home.

A knock on the ceiling.

Bob   Sod!

Bob *goes out.* **Mother** *looks round in tiredness and fatigue.* **Mrs Wilson** *comes in with tea things.*

Mrs Wilson   Where's Bob?

Mother (*looks at ceiling. Vaguely*)   Knockin'.

Mrs Wilson   Mr Wilson, my husband. Sit down. You look worn out. (*Lays the table.*) Some of them lose interest towards the end. No trouble with his appetite. I can't begrudge what I put on the plate. I'll be out of pocket. I was surprised how little Lord Are was willing to pay. It's much nicer here than in the cells next door. (*Pours one cup of tea.*) If he gets off (O I'm sure he will) Mr Wilson loses his hanging money. This was supposed to make up the loss – which means it'll add to it.

Mother   Thankyoo.

Mrs Wilson   Mr Wilson's poorly. They say it's nothing but I know better. Those two are like father and son. Soon's Bob hears the rap he's up those stairs, rattling away. I don't say. D'you eat turf cakes? I made these little ones. There. I'm not the sort of person to count what they put on the plate. Five.

Mother   Thankyoo.

Mrs Wilson   His turns get worse. Passed the age for outside work.

Bob *comes in.*

Mrs Wilson   Try not to clank dear. My head's been arguing with me all morning. We're down to three. I don't suppose we'll eat them all. Why didn't you offer your mother a chair, you rude boy? I don't mind who uses them.

Bob *writes on a corner of the table.*

Mrs Wilson   Mr Wilson daren't give the job up, even I can't manage on what he makes next door. I like to have things round me, otherwise what is there to show? A change of curtains. Proper tea things but that lid's cracked. A few pairs of Sunday gloves. They stick out a mile when everyone puts their hands up to pray.

Mother   Thankyoo.

Mrs Wilson   I'll put the tin beside the plate. Then what we don't eat can jump back. Help yourself. (*She pushes the plate further away.*) They ought to bring it indoors. Out all weathers. No wonder he has turns. The better class tip. But you can't rely. Even if I know he's got a busy week I can't say 'I'll go out and buy that new teapot.' (*To* **Bob**.) What was it this time?

Bob (*writing*)   Hand shook an' splash his shirt. Had to howd his cup.

Mrs Wilson   O don't tell me he's having one of those. Eat your turf cake.

Bob   Ont hungry.

Mrs Wilson   O a mood is it?

Bob   No.

Mrs Wilson   Don't have moods in my house. We set the cat on them. Well when you ask it'll be gone. (*She eats his cake.*)

Knock on ceiling.

Bob   Drat! Forgot his Bible.

Mrs Wilson   What are our young people coming to? Fancy forgetting a Bible!

Bob *takes the Bible from under a chair.*

Mrs Wilson *(calls)*   Bible's on its way. – You are a funny lad at times. *(To* **Mother**.*)* It occupies his mind when he's like this. He writes all the births and baptisms and weddings in the front –

Bob *goes out with the Bible.*

Mrs Wilson   – and his work in the back. Goes through them to soothe his mind. I'll clear away, there are light-fingered gentlemen around. I'll wrap that cake with the bite in the side. I believe that was you. It'll do for the way back.

Mother *(gently tugs* **Mrs Wilson**'s *sleeve)*   His wife's outside. It preys on his mind.

Mr Hardache *comes in.*

Hardache   Mrs Hedges. Ma'am. His lordship's here.

Bob *comes in.*

Hardache   Say nothing Bob. A harmless prank and you were the engine of fate. Here's half a guinea.

Mrs Wilson   Half a guinea.

Bob   Thanks. *(Gives it to* **Mother**.*)* Rose have that.

Mrs Wilson   Mr Hedges you're as thoughtless as my guests next door. Now what have you got for tips?

Are *and* **Parson** *come in.*

Are   Bob, these are better –

Bob   Rose ont allowed in.

Are   You'll see her soon.

Bob   Rather see her now. Goo back to the cell if thass necessary.

Are   Surly Bob, do not abuse my trust.

Bob   Ont hev her stood in the street.

Are   Ye make it deuced awkward for your friends Bob. Fetch her, Parson.

Bob   Hev yoo my pardon sir?

Are   I have it not on me, but 'tis safe. There's a style to these things Bob. 'Tis not unknown for it to be held back till the man comes to the scaffold.

Hardache (*taking* **Are** *to one side*)   We have a little business to settle.

Are   What Mr Hardache?

Hardache   Your murder of my daughter.

Are   Bob, show your mother your letters.

Mother   Letters. There! I shall hev a readin' an' writin' son.

Mother *and* **Bob** *sit at the table.*

Are (*to* **Hardache**)   The black slut? – Father-in-law you did not build your empire by listening to trash.

Hardache   Wrong lad, I listened to it very well. I call you lad because I noticed you've started to call me father. I don't like interfering – but she was my daughter and she'd want the right man to hang.

Bob   I writ Rose. Parson can mix the letters up to spell eros – an' that, he say, is the lower form of love.

Hardache   Son-in-law, here's a riddle: why does a sensible man like me let his daughter marry a fop like you?

Are   Fop?

Hardache   Coal.

Are   I misheard.

Hardache   No. Under your land.

Are   I have been rooked.

Hardache   Your title cost me a packet but I meant to pay for it with your coal. The marriage made it mine. Or my grandson's – I think ahead for the good of the firm. Now this mishap upsets my grand scheme.

Are   Why didn't my steward tell me I had coal?

Hardache   I paid him not to.

Are   Father-in-law you are Father Satan.

Hardache   Ay well you meant that as flattery but happen when you know me better you'll think it's deserved. (*Document.*) Here's a simple agreement of intent. Our lawyers will work out the details. All what's over your land is yours: that goes for the late Lady Are's money. What's under is mine: barrin' your ancestors' bones. Sign, and my daughter can sleep in peace for a very long time.

Are   Bob lend me thy pen.

Bob   Expect a pardon look like that.

Hardache   Happen it does for some.

Are (*signs*)   This day I sign an alliance with the Devil.

Rose *comes in.* **Bob** *embraces her.*

Bob   Ont mind if the people see our joy, all's friends here.

Mother   Can't stay long Rose. Miss the cart back.

Rose   Mr Hardache did you go to the court?

Hardache   Lass I considered it but it won't wear.

Are *leaves.* **Mother** *collects her things and goes to the door.*

Hardache   You offer no witness. Bob can show me his pardon when it comes. I'll see he's set up in a good way. Let's leave the youngsters to their peace.

All go except **Bob** *and* **Rose**.

Rose   I'm going outside, climb on the wall of the gaol and shout, 'Are is a murderer.'

Bob   Rose he promise –

Rose   He promised they wouldn't find you guilty.

Bob   He explained. Can't buy a whole jury. Look, his mother old Lady Are was the king's whore or summat. She's got the pardon in the bag.

Rose   I've got money. We could get that chain off –

Bob (*removes leg from fetter*)   Thass only for show.

Rose   God! There's a fast coach to Lynn! We'll be on the boat tonight!

Bob   Thass madness! I git caught I git hang!

Rose   You are caught! Bob the door's open. If it was shut yer could kick it down. Yer could push the wall down. You're strong. But yer sit and wait to be hanged.

Bob   How do I love thee Rose. When I ont git a pardon, then I'll speak out!

Rose   Too late.

Bob   I am an Englishman, a freeborn Englishman. I hev a right to speak – to shout for all to hear! Thass in our law. Stand up – in court, the street corner, top of the roof – an' shout the truth. It must be so!

Rose   You're a slave but don't know it. My mother *saw* her chains. How can yer fight for freedom when yer think you've got it? Yer won't go, if there was a chance he'd put yer a mile underground an' chain yer to the wall. Then yer'd be free: yer'd know what you are.

Rose *goes out.*

Bob   All my life I struggled. Bob the joker. Bob the sport. Walk down the road, sun shines, eat, work – struggle to keep body and soul together. Yoo got yoor strength, Bob, yoo can do anythin'. Where did I goo wrong? Long ago I should hev put my boot in their teeth every time the bastards smiled at me. I've left it late. Now it's dark. Black. Black. Black. I must goo

steady, or make a terrible blunder. I must trust the clown an'
hope for my reward.

ONCE ARMIES MET (**Bob**)

Once armies met in the field to fight
One was wrong and one was right
They fought all day – they fought all night
The dead were dead but would not depart
And war would not go away

War was between the future and past
The newborn smile and the senile mind
War was the bloody formal dance
Of red-liveried cannon-fodder
To the music of mankind

Now an army watches with ten thousand eyes
It cannot see the suicide-man
In his everyday casual high-street disguise
Or scan the marks on his city plan
The dead are dead and the living wait
And war has not gone away

And you – you march in the city street
Shouting 'Out! Out! Out!' and 'Not in my name!'
That's just playing the anti-war game
When you don't know how to make peace

When you don't know how to make peace
The dead will still die
Day in and day out
And war will not go away

What is the price of peace?
What will you give so the dead may live
And war be sent away?

It is the price you refuse to pay!
Hypocrite dealers in anger and hate
You want war to stay and not go away
You say justice belongs to another day?
And tell the dead they can wait!

Scene Nine

London. **Old Lady Are***'s house. Drawing room.*

Rose *and* **Old Lady Are**.

Old Lady Are *in a chair. On the floor, across the room, a decanter.*

Rose   They say my husband murdered your daughter-in-law.

Lady Are   I shall send him a guinea.

Rose   My husband didn't kill her.

Lady Are   D'you like fish? It lures me with the passion that drives youth to its follies. I ate too much at dinner. (*Points.*) My glass child. My maid Dorothea, the vixen, puts it out of my reach.

Rose (*hands her the glass*)   Your son killed her.

Lady Are   My son? O I've slopped the glass! (*Chokes.*) Dear me. Thump my back child. (**Rose** *pats her back.*) Thump I say! Lay on! O 'tis good! The seizure will take me. (*Wipes her eyes.*) Swear 'tis true! I must have my coach at dawn to tell the town.

Rose   I was afraid you wouldn't believe me.

Lady Are   Believe ye? 'Tis the easiest thing to believe! I can't tip your husband – but you shall have the guinea.

Rose   Lord Are says you've got us a pardon.

Lady Are   Pox on the rogue! I haven't seen him since the day his father died. He snatched the pillow from under his head, bounded downstairs (one at a time, he had heels on), threw it at me, yowlped 'Hurrah!' and hounded me from the house. (*Drinks.*) Come, see. (*Takes a huge pile of papers from her bosom.*) Shares, letters, promissory notes. All his. (*Wheezes as she fondles the papers.*) Look, forty thousand pounds. (*Paper.*) A half-share in Jamaica. (*Paper.*) That would pay for his pox pills. (*Paper.*) A castle in Scotland. (*Kisses papers and puts them back in her dress.*) Home to my heart, darlings. (*Paper.*) A letter from the Prime Minister to the Primate of England. You could blackmail him with this till he had to raise the income tax to pay you – and still have the Primate's reply. (*Laughs and stuffs papers away.*) Back to the bosom that gave him suck (one Wednesday when the wet nurse was late) but now makes amends by making him starve. (*Smoothes her dress.*) They go with me to the grave and angels do not lie on softer down.

Rose   He says the pardon's already –

Lady Are   Pardon, pardon – cease with your pardons! My glass. There are no pardons.

Rose   But you can get one?

Lady Are   'Tis true my figure sets a fashion few could follow – but the prince always liked a lady of carriage. He'd bed me still but his flesh is wore out with paint. His servants carry him round the palace in a sedan chair. He looks out of the window like a monkey sticking out of its jungle. A pardon? – nothing would be easier. 'Twould be as if the monkey reached up, plucked a banana from a tree and threw it into my lap. But I shall not ask.

Rose   Lady Are my husband's innocent!

Lady Are   True, but he hath put out that he is not. Let him hang for a boaster and go to heaven. If he stays in this world he will go to hell with the rest of the footmen. Pardon? Ye might as well ask me to lead a riot or open a revolution.

Rose   My husband is good and kind and –

Lady Are   I like him more and more.

Rose (*kneels*)   I beg you.

Lady Are   Get up child. A thing is not made more impressive by being said by a dwarf. The ground is what we have risen from. Up! Ye made an old lady merry with a farce and now ye mar it with a wailing play!

Rose   You bitch! I hope you choke! Die of gin! Have yer head cracked with yer bottle! An' get pox from yer monkey!

Rose *goes.*

Lady Are   The wretch hath a tongue on her like Dorothea, but she would have stayed for the guinea. I forgot to get the details! (*Calls.*) Dorothea! – Coupling with the kitchen boy again? Hush, I'll invent the details. 'Twas at table. She empties his plate on his head, the gravy streams down his French coat and he runs her through and slips on a pudding and turns and cartwheels while she – O! Ho! Ha! (*Laughs and wheezes.*) Her – her – O! I shall be in bed for a week! Peace think of something else! – her last breath blows bubbles in the soup! (*She laughs.*) O! Hoo! Ha! (*Stops. Suddenly afraid.*) The cold wind round my heart . . . The turbot. The cream sauce. The doctor forbade it. (*Wipes her mouth.*) . . . I am an old woman with an empty glass and there is nothing to think of that does not wring me with regret for the past, convulse me at the follies of the present, or make me tremble before what is to come. I have not always lived after the precepts. 'Twould do no harm to prepare for heaven. Pah! a morbid thought. 'Twould drive my son to hell – that is heaven, and I shall be the *deus ex machina* in it. As in the old romances, he shall be reprieved at the tree. I shall send a copy direct to that scoundrel my son to give him the misery of reading it.

THE FAIR TREE OF LIBERTY (**Rose** *and* **Frank**)

On the fair tree of liberty
The fruit weighs the branches to the ground
And look! the fruit are eyes
At the stealthy tread they open to see
The robber who comes to rob the tree
He turns around and runs
The eyes are brighter than a hundred suns

On the fair tree of liberty
The fruit weighs the branches to the ground
And look! the fruit are eyes
At the marching tread they open to see
The axeman who comes to fell the tree
He turns around and runs
The eyes are brighter than a hundred suns

On the fair tree of liberty
The fruit weighs the branches to the ground
And look! the fruit are eyes
At the heavy tread they open to see
The headsman who comes to burn the tree
He turns around and runs
The eyes are brighter than a hundred suns

Deep in the trunk bees murmur like thunder
High in the crown birds call
Telling the names of the passers-by
The eyes watch them as they come
And sometimes the branches rise and strike them down
  like bolts of thunder

And so the fair tree grows
As tall as the pine and strong as the oak
Wreathed with the climbing honeysuckle
The wild rose and the hanging vine
As our forefathers spoke

Scene Ten

Hilgay. The Hall. Breakfast room.

Are. *For the first time he is seen in a shirt and breeches and without a wig.*

Are   Let a man have a fine day for his hanging. An empty house, all gone for the best places. How pleasantly the sun shines in at my windows to bless me.

Mother *comes in.*

Mother   Gentleman. Say it's urgent. Hev a letter.

Are   O let him deliver. 'Tis a small cloud, 'twill pass.

Mother *goes.*

Are   Now to the business of the day: clothes. (*Sighs.*) I shall be glad when the day is past, when those who are to suffer have suffered and the rest may enjoy themselves as the world desires, without the mournful countenance a Christian must spoil his hat with on these occasions.

Mother *comes in with the* **Messenger**. *She goes.*

Messenger   My lord, your mother's compliments.

Are   Damme the she-goat repents!

The **Messenger** *hands* **Are** *a document.* **Are** *reads it.*

Are   Handsome. So Bob has his good news at last. To think he lieth in his pains and I hold in my hand his absolute liberty. 'Tis feathers to a bird.

Messenger   I must go to the prison.

Are   Prison?

Messenger   That is a copy. I am commissioned to hand the original to the governor.

Are   Lookee there is a great crowd about the roads. I'll take thee in my coach.

Messenger   'Tis kind my lord, but I am commissioned to −

Are   Commission the pox! Would ye deny me my pleasure?

Messenger   Yes sir. I am commissioned to take −

Are   But now I think on't I cannot take ye. I have my Lady Oxy to sit beside me and her mother the Duchess of Blare to sit opposite and the Duchess will have Lucille her maid. Now Lucille is an absolute termagant, an hysteric who rules the Duchess with a rod of iron and will have no man near her. The Duchess was on the point of saying I must run behind and hang onto the strap.

He has poured two cups of coffee. He hands one to the **Messenger** *and drinks the other.*

Are   No sir do not ask: ye may *not* sit on the roof. That's booked by Lady Oxy's boys and their chums − for the boys will go to the hangings. We shall have such a hallooing and hurrahing as we fly through the lanes, such a stamping of feet on the roof, such a throwing of the coachman's hat into the duckponds ('tis only a matter of lettin' 'em grow up before we go to *their* hangin') –

Messenger *laughs.*

Are   – that Lucille will have hysterics, sniff two bottles of smelling salts dry and must lie down, miss the hangings and have the Duchess fan her (the poor lady is tyrannised, 'tis a scandal – and blackmail is rumoured) so that we hear nothing but the maid's complaints all the way back, when the rest of the company (in the natural circle of friendship) wish to give their versions of the last confession, in one of which he will protest he is as innocent as the unborn lamb and in another claim to have been a highwayman from the age of ten. No sir I will not take ye in the coach for the journey there will be so like the journey to hell ye'd change places with Bob sooner than enter it for the journey back. Yet my conscience fears ye will not get through the mob.

Messenger (*putting the cup on the table*)   As to that sir, I'll shout 'Clear in the King's name!'

Are   Never do that! Nay if ye shout that I cannot let ye through the door. They will suspect ye bring a pardon and pull ye from your horse. 'Twould spoil their day. When a man's hanged the rest of the day's theirs, for riot or sober reflection. When he is not, they work.

Messenger   I'm grateful for the warning sir. Now my commission must –

Are   Wait! (*Aside.*) Must I kill another before breakfast? I shall run out of Bobs.

Messenger   Good day sir –

Are   I have it! I have it! I cannot take you in my coach – but I may take the pardon.

Messenger   But sir my commission says –

Are   Sir you surprise me! Thou hast dawdled long enough.
More delay and I must complain to thy officer. Here are thirty
guineas in gold.

Messenger   Thirty guineas!

Are   'Tis naught. Fly to the tavern and drink my health. 'Tis
a commission. God bless thee. I must dress and jump about.

Messenger   I thank your lordship.

The **Messenger** *gives* **Are** *the pardon and goes.*

Are   Now sure I am looked on by a guardian angel – though
from whence I know not! I hold in my hand his pardon. I shall
not deliver it. What, no thunder? The sun does not stop in its
course! Lookee Are: thou art a strange soul. I begin to like
thee, and I might worship thee. Ye have talents, nay powers
I knew not of! Why d'ye live in poverty and marry an ash-
raker's daughter? Why have ye not twenty houses? A hundred
women? An army? Ye fear Lord this and fawn on Lady that,
ye hack your way down the street with your cane – when ye
might be carried along it on the backs of the mob! All shall
change. There shall be a new world. (*Calls.*) Hedges! Lay out
my blue coat and yellow hat. Nay, my pink with purple plumes.
Let us not add to Bob's woes: he shall see a good hat at his
hanging. Let the Great Boob hang to prove the world's in its
senses. Besides, 'tis heartless to deny a mob. *Noblesse oblige*: hang
him.

Yet I grow fond! Think, I cannot ride up with the pardon!
I must forgo the hanging! I take not the coach. I say I go
horseback to go faster. On the way I fall. Racing and hollooing
with the joy of glad tidings, over I go tippity-top – knocked
out. When I get to my feet the jade hath run. (I shall whip her
off. 'Tis a faithful beast and will cling – but I'll break my whip
on her and throw stones.) Then I have my limp. (*Practises.*) Nay,
severer. (*Practises as he talks.*) I hobble (I have cut a stick from the
hedge) to a nearby farm. Deserted. All at the hanging. We have
not seen such desolation since the Black Death. On I crawl.
Till time hath run out and poor Bob the Boob is led under the

tree. He looks up at heaven – in the direction of the parson's finger – to the welcoming face of God: and all he sees is the black beam above him. I sit in the hedge and weep. Yea, I uncover my head and kneel in the nettles and pray: for the rope to break.

O great blazing sun! Great fire of everlasting day! My life! My ministering star! Blaze! Blaze! Blaze! Blaze! Hail great light, orb of the world that I shall stride in! . . . O my friends –

Mother *comes in.*

Mother   Blue an' pink's laid out.

Are   Hedges. Rest in thy chamber.

Mother   Keep busy. Cry for him last night, cry later.

Are   Mothers know best. Lookee, light a fire against my return. The day might yet be cold. Warm thy old hands at the blaze. Here is a paper to start it.

Are *gives her the pardons. He goes.*

Mother   Kind on him. Save me fetch the kindlin'. Official. Pretty crown on top. (*Shakes her head.*) Bob was learnin' to read. (*Tears the papers.*)

Mother *starts the fire.*

Are (*off*)   Hedges!

Mother (*sighing to herself as she stoops – she has become much older*) Now what?

Are *comes in, shouting.*

Are   'Tis too much! Hedges will ye make me a fool! Dress me in motley? Set me up as a clown?

Mother (*calm, flat*)   Sir whatever is the –

Are   Damned impertinence! Can a man trust nothing! Are you blind?

Mother (*calm, flat*)   Now sir I'm sure there's no call to –

Are   No, ye did it on purpose! Petty revenge! (*Holds out his blue coat.*) Where is the button! D'ye see it? No! 'Tis off! (*Throws his blue coat on the floor.*) Here, here (*Thumps his chest.*) where every fool can see it! You ancient hag must I sew it myself? I give ye the roof over your head, the ground under your feet, the food on your plate – for a gaping hole with two black spots and a white thread like the lower-anatomy of a mouse! An idiot's badge!

Mother   Give it here, I'll see to –

Are   Now? When it lies in the filth? I must dress like a tramp! O she will sew the button now the coat can't be worn! (*Kicks the coat.*) Madam sew it on and throw the coat in the kennels for my bitch to whelp on. Let her at least have the respect of a full set of buttons. (*Suddenly becomes his old self again.*) Now I must wear my green. So I cannot wear my pink. 'Twould look like a maypole. I must wear my yellow – which I wore twice at the races. (*Aside.*) 'Tis true I can't go to the hanging. But now the whole country will say 'twas because I could not afford a new hat!

Are goes. **Mother** *mutters to herself as she goes back to the fire.*

Mother   Can't sew it. Ont give me the button.

SUDDENLY (**Bob**)

It came suddenly like a bomb
They didn't die with the gestures of dying
They didn't cover their heads in fear
They didn't lift their hands in supplication
They died with the gestures of living

It came suddenly like a bomb
Mouths were open but the words were not spoken
The salt was lifted but wasn't shaken
They died with the gestures of living
Fingers beckoned and hands stretched out to feel
Heads leaned forward in concentration
On words they would never hear

So sudden was the disaster
So swift the moment of fate
It fell at the time of the midday meal
When the fork was halfway between
The mouth and the plate

Scene Eleven

Peterborough. Holme Cottage. Kitchen. A beer barrel.

Mrs Wilson *and* **Bob**.

Bob *is in shirtsleeves and without fetters. He drinks at the table.*

Bob   When woman?

Mrs Wilson *fills his glass. He grabs her arms.*

Bob   She's a sly one.

Mrs Wilson   Behave or I'll tell Mr Wilson.

Bob (*lets her arm go*)   His nibs is quiet. He'll hev to come down
for my pardon.

Mrs Wilson   Let him sleep.

Bob (*shouts at the ceiling*)   Who's in the Land of Nod? Shh!

Mrs Wilson   On your feet. Put your jacket on.

Bob (*stands, staggers slightly, steadies himself with one hand on the
table*)   Phew. Powerful stuff.

Mrs Wilson (*buttons*)   Fasten you in.

Bob   Us'll shake hands. Thankyoo sir. (*Giggles.*) Think when
they see how posh I am they most likely give me two pardons.

Mrs Wilson   I'll top you up.

Bob (*flat palm over the glass*)   Nope. Ont drink n'more.

Parson *and* **Rose** *come in.*

Bob   Rose! My gal. How I hev miss you. (*Kiss.*) There – the terrible times are over. (*Whispers to* **Rose**.) Mrs Wilson says it's come today. Sh! – Parson yoo let your faith wobble but yoo'll git a surprise. Mrs Wilson do the man the honours an' pour his drink. (*Wipes the glass clean on his sleeve.*) Drat spoil me coat. (*Hands the glass to* **Mrs Wilson**.) The letters swim in my head like thass a shipwreck.

Parson (*low*)   Mrs Wilson to do this at such an hour is cruel. Wrong. A needless adding to his burdens.

Mrs Wilson   I don't need a sermon on how to run a gaol. The profit I make on this it's not worth buying in. (*Gives him the glass.*) No doubt you'll take your glass Parson?

Parson (*slight embarrassment*)   Yes, yes, thank you. His and my way go differently today.

Mrs Wilson *keeps a tally of the beer that is drunk. She marks it on a slate with chalk.*

Bob   Rose is ought wrong?

She has her back to him. He turns her round. Her face is showered in tears. He steps back.

That . . . ont tears of joy . . . (*Vaguely.*) Why'm I wearin' my best jacket?

Parson (*hands him an open prayer book*)   Read your prayers to me.

Bob   Ont want a lesson!

Mrs Wilson (*to* **Rose**)   Hand me his glass.

Bob   Ay! Less drink! Sorry Parson. Why's this gloom fall all around? Rose I only lent his lordship my name.

The **Parson** *has three prayer books open at 'The Burial of the Dead'. He reads and recites Psalm 39 continuously (interrupting himself only once) and the rest of the scene goes on round him. He finally stops reading when he says 'At last. Better. He comes to thee.' After that he prays silently. As the* **Parson** *reads from his own book he offers* **Bob** *the* *second book, open at the place.* **Bob** *snatches this and throws it on the ground.*

Bob   Ont pray at me! Ont be hanged!

The **Parson** *picks up the book while he reads his own.*

Bob   Drunk! (*Empties his drink on the floor but does not throw the mug.*)

Mrs Wilson   O I see we're going to have one of those days. – He should have been told properly. It's not decent treating him like this. – Bobby sit down. Crying won't help.

Bob (*stares at* **Mrs Wilson**)   Woman what yoo done? . . . Yoo towd me my pardon was . . . (*Sudden idea.*) Ah!

Bob *lurches out.* **Mrs Wilson** *goes on her knees and mops up the beer.*

Mrs Wilson   Mrs Hedges stand by him or go outside.

Rose   He's innocent.

Mrs Wilson   They all are if you listen long enough.

Crash upstairs.

There goes the door. That'll cost someone. All this fuss! You come here and behave as if I had nothing better to do.

Crash upstairs.

(*Shouting up.*) You wicked boy!

Bob (*off*)   Ah!

Mrs Wilson   There'll be the dickens to pay.

Bob (*off*)   Bed made. Cold.

Gaoler *comes in with* **Frank**.

Frank *is drunk.*

Gaoler   Cart's outside ma'am. Jist git the horse in.

Frank (*singing – morose, almost inaudible*)
    Old Samson had a daughter, her name was Isabelle
    The lily of the valley and the primrose of the dell

When she went a-walking she choosed me for her guide
Down by the Arun river to watch the fishes glide

(*Sees* **Bob** *through the door.*) Two of Bob. Have to hang twice.

Bob *comes in.*

Bob   So I'm to hang. Skinned alive. Rose what'll us do? (*Tries to think. Turns to* **Parson***.*) Howd his row or I crack his head!

Parson *prays uninterruptedly.*

Gaoler   Goo quiet or goo shackled, you hev the choice. (*Pours drinks and raises glass.*) Drink to both gents. Wish I could drink to better times. (*Drinks.*)

Bob   Curses! That a man dies so! Git Are here! That blackguard! Why doo he doo this? Touch cap – work quiet – bow – ont that enough? Now he want my head!

Frank
The first three months were scarcely o'er
The youngest gal lost her bloom
The red fell from her bonny cheeks
And her eyes began to swoon

Bob   Yes Frank sing! Kiss me Rose. Yoo ont ashamed of me. How I doo love thee! Ont miss the world: miss thee. (*Jumps onto the table.*) Shall we hang? Then hang so high?

Points up. **Frank** *tries to climb onto the table with him.*

Bob *and* **Frank**
The next nine months was passed and gone
She brought forth to me a son
And I was quickly sent for
To see what could be done

Frank (*continues alone*)
I said I should marry her
But o! that would not be

Parson (*tapping* **Frank** *on the back*)   My friend open your heart –

Frank   Git off me yer sinful old bugger! I'll open you!

Frank *snatches the prayer books and throws them away.*

The **Gaoler** *moves in. The* **Parson** *motions him back. He closes his eyes and goes on reciting the prayers aloud by heart.* **Bob** *notices nothing of this but comes down from the table.*

Mrs Wilson (*pouring beer*)   Four. I keep count so no one's overcharged. (*To* **Rose**.) They're allowed one in the cart. I'd offer, but now there's the door to pay . . . (*Pours drinks for everyone.*)

DRUM SONG (**Bob**)

A drummer beat upon a drum
And no sound came
He hit the skin
He struck the skin
And no sound came
Wild in his frenzy
A madman sweating blood
He beat he struck he hammered blows
And no sound came
He thrashed and lashed
All through the night
And on into the light
Till his hands bled
Till his eyes bled
Till blood ran from his ears
Till the teeth shook in his head
Till the bones rattled in his body like dice
And still he made no sound
He struck with sticks of iron
With sticks of bone
With sticks of steel
He staggered
He began to reel
In pain
He hammered on
Again! Again!

He crawled upon the ground
He flailed the drum lashed to his side
And no sound came
From the beaten hide
He did not stop till he was dead
   And other men are silent
   When they labour them
   About the head

Bob   The pardon'll come on the square. Rose I'm scared to die. (*Holds her.*)

Parson   At last. Better. He comes to thee. (*Kneels and prays silently.*)

Frank   God rot yer Bobby Hedges! I'll pay to go second an' see yer swing. There's justice in this! I hope yer hanging's a cruel one. Yer live to cry mercy on the rope an' don't get it! Yer dragged me to the gallows, yer rantin' hypocrite!

He falls down.

Gaoler (*calling to outside*)   She playin' yoo up?

Rose   Drink. (*Gets glass.*) Bobby.

Bob *takes the glass and gulps it down.* **Mrs Wilson** *refills* **Bob***'s glass and holds him as* **Rose** *pours it into his mouth.*

Parson   Mrs Wilson I'll lodge a complaint.

Gaoler *picks* **Frank** *up and lays him over the barrel.*

Rose (*tilts* **Bob***'s head back and pours drink down his throat*) Drink. Drink. Drink.

Parson   No! Let him feel the pain or God's anger is not slaked!

Mrs Wilson (*to* **Bob**)   Mr Wilson will help you. It doesn't take long.

Gaoler (*calling to the outside*)   Ready?

Bob (*pushing the glass away*)   No. Ont. Clear head. Speak. In square. Innocent. Englishman. Are's murderer. Murder me. English.

Parson   Nay! Who can believe a man who speaks so harshly against his lord? Have you no gratitude?

Bob   Ay? Ay? Gratitude they want? . . . What can I say? . . . Who'll hear all I can say?

Gaoler   Pay no heed, Parson. They say all sorts − (*To* **Bob**.) and out there no one listen. They'll shortly give yoo cause to wish yoo'd saved yoor breath.

Voice (*off*)   She's in.

Bob (*shakes his head to clear it. Then to audience*)   I ont believe this.

Gaoler *takes* **Bob** *and* **Frank** *out.* **Frank** *sings. The* **Parson** *picks up the three prayer books and puts on his last vestments as he follows the others out.*

Mrs Wilson (*to* **Rose**)   You can lie down upstairs. Bed's made. Clear this mess away. Wish Mr Wilson didn't have to go out today. When he's had a turn he's nervous. That young man's just waiting to step into his shoes.

Rose *has followed the others out.* **Mrs Wilson** *checks the amount she has sold.*

Scene Twelve

London Bridge.

Rose.

Rose   I stand on London Bridge. Bodies float in the sky and sink towards the horizon. Crocodiles drift in the Thames. On the embankment the plane trees rattle their fingers. Men walk the city streets with chains hanging from their mouths. Pillars of black smoke rise between the towers and the temples. The stars will come out like scabs on the sky.

MAN IS WHAT HE KNOWS (**Rose**)

Does the judge say
I send your arms to prison today
But your feet are free
To walk away?

Does the boss buy
The apple core from the market stall
And leave the skin?
He buys it all

Do the troops shoot
To kill your stomach but not your head?
They shoot to kill
You drop down dead

Once Satan roamed the earth to find
Souls that money could buy
Now he comes to steal your mind
He doesn't wait till you die

Man is what he knows – or doesn't know
The empty men reap death and sow
Famine wherever they march
But they do not own the earth
Sooner believe I could strike it a blow
With my fist and miss!

Geese fly over the moon and do not know
    That for a moment they fill the world with beauty
Flakes do not know where they fall in the snow
    Wind and rain cannot tell where they blow
But we may know who we are and where we go

I cross the bridge and go into the city streets.

Made in the USA
San Bernardino, CA
26 January 2019